Exploring

HEAVENLY PLACES

THE MYSTERY OF THE ANCIENT PATHS

VOLUME 12

Thus says the Lord: "Stand by the roads, and look, and ask for the ancient paths, where the good way is; and walk in it, and find rest for your souls. (Jeremiah 6:16a)

exploring

HEAVENLY PLACES

THE MYSTERY OF THE ANCIENT PATHS

VOLUME 12

By

Paul L. Cox

Barbara Kain Parker

EXPLORING HEAVENLY PLACES, VOLUME 12

THE MYSTERY OF THE ANCIENT PATHS

By Paul L. Cox and Barbara Kain Parker

Aslan's Place Publications
9315 Sagebrush Street
Apple Valley, CA 92308
760-810-0990
aslansplace.com

Unless otherwise indicated, scriptures are taken from the: The ESV® Bible (The Holy Bible, English Standard Version®) copyright © 2001 by Crossway Bible, a publishing ministry of Good News Publishers. Used by permission. All rights reserved.

Printed in the United States of America

PREFACE

Exploring Heavenly Places, Volume 12 is being written in the midst of a national stay-at-home advisory during the Coronavirus pandemic. Our research has been in the works for months, but the book simply wasn't coming together. I had no idea about how to begin, and despite a long, potential outline nothing seemed quite right. Then, during a recent Lion's Den broadcast,[1] I finally had my ah-ha moment and the pieces finally began falling into place. You see, the book couldn't be written until recent revelatory information was received, which rounds out the message the Lord has given us to share.

By the time this book is published, the pandemic will hopefully be history; but as Jesus foretold, the latter days, or end times, will be rife with terrible and frightening events. Even so, His promise remains certain:

> *Peace I leave with you; my peace I give to you. Not as the world gives do I give to you. Let not your hearts be troubled, neither let them be afraid.*[2]

Contrary to many media reports, Christianity is not against science. Rather, much of mainstream media hates Christianity and denies God's righteousness; it denies the

---

[1] Webinars or podcasts sharing latest information from Aslan's Place: aslansplace.com/lionsden/
[2] John 14:27

reality of His truth regarding the spiritual world, which the Bible identifies as the heavenly places. Oh, fictional supernatural thrillers and super heroes are fine, but in the physical realm our supernatural God is unwelcome by many.

During this stressful time, a few of the not-so-helpful suggested coping mechanisms I've read include:

- Embrace the resiliency of life; after all, regardless of what happens human life will continue and years from now this will be just a distant memory
- Take a deep breath, hold it for ten seconds and release it slowly to alleviate some of your fears
- Burdensome to-do and not-to-do lists of things that will lessen your anxiety

Regardless of the advice, unless biblically based, it all seems to come down to a Ralph Waldo Emerson quote, "Nobody can bring you peace but yourself." Not true! Peace is not a place; it's not a state of mind that one achieves; peace is a person, and His name is Jesus Christ:

> *For to us a child is born, to us a son is given; and the government shall be upon his shoulder, and his name shall be called Wonderful Counselor, Mighty Everlasting Father, Prince of Peace. Of the increase of his government and of peace there will be no end, on the throne of David and over his kingdom to establish it and to uphold it with justice and with*

righteousness from this time forth and forevermore.
The zeal of the Lord of hosts will do this.[3]

May the content of this book serve to encourage the Church for years to come, regardless of life's current trial. The fact is, God never changes and regardless of whatever comes our way, He is sufficient in every circumstance.[4]

Barbara Kain Parker

---

[3] Isaiah 9:6-7
[4] 2 Corinthians 12:9

TABLE OF CONTENTS

INTRODUCTION

Some time ago, Paul realized that four little words tend to dominate our lives after the Lord repeated them to him over and over throughout the night. Those words: want, need, lack and expect. However, that focus does nothing to bolster the attitude by which we should be living; it is contrary to everything Jesus taught. Sadly, instead of seeking Him first we tend to concentrate all too often on everyday stuff. How easily we seem to forget the admonition:

Set your minds on things that are above, not on things that are on earth.[1]

Key to overcoming the ravenous appetite of worldly expectations is a biblical understanding of what they should be as opposed to what they often are. We also need insights regarding how our warped perceptions of want, need, lack and expect came to be in the first place.

Our goal for this volume of *Exploring Heavenly Places* is to further equip God's people to persevere and endure within a worldly system that wants nothing more than to snuff out Christianity. We offer suggestions that lead to a greater understanding of the *The Mystery of the Ancient Paths*; we offer hope because that is exactly what our Lord offers:

---

[1] Colossians 3:2

11

Have you not known? Have you not heard? The Lord is the everlasting God, the Creator of the ends of the earth. He does not faint or grow weary; his understanding is unsearchable. He gives power to the faint, and to him who has no might he increases strength. Even youths shall faint and be weary, and young men shall fall exhausted; but they who wait for the Lord shall renew their strength; they shall mount up with wings like eagles; they shall run and not be weary; they shall walk and not faint.[2]

As in some recent editions of the *Exploring Heavenly Places* series, first-person references (I, me, my) refer to Barbara; all of Paul's words are clearly indicated by name.

Paul L. Cox
Barbara Kain Parker

---

[2] Isaiah 40:28-31

CHAPTER ONE:

THE REST OF THE LORD

Many years ago, the Lord began teaching Paul about entering into God's rest, and in subsequent years he has taught and written about it. Since rest is a vital component of surviving the times, we are re-visiting portions of Paul's article, *Entering the Rest of the Lord:*[1]

I had a sermon that I felt God had matured in me about the glory of God. Very early in my Baptist days, I'd preached through the book of Exodus and came to the passage where Moses said, "Lord, show me Your glory." The reason he had said it was that God was angry at the people because He looked down and saw them sacrificing to idols; they were sacrificing their children. They didn't just sacrifice grain and fruit; in that culture you sacrificed babies…and God said, "I want you to go down and deal with that."

So Moses went down the mountain and he saw it. He became angry, and then he and God had a talk. God said, "Now, Moses, what are you going to do with your people?" And Moses answered, "They are not my people; they are Your people." God replied, "Well, I'm just going to wipe them out." So Moses argued, "God, you can't do that. What is

---

[1] aslansplace.com/entering-the-rest-of-the-lord-paul-l-cox/

going to happen to Your name, to Your fame? What are people going to think about You? Are they going to say, 'You're the kind of God that brings somebody out of Egypt and then You kill them all?'"

So he contended with God. He laid hold of God, and God was not budging until finally Moses went for the ultimate prayer, "Lord, show me Your glory." I preached on this. And right about now you're probably thinking, "What does that have to do with what we have just been talking about?" Read on.

The Lord answered immediately, "Yes, I will show you My glory." He put Moses in the cleft of the rock and His glory passed by; then He started proclaiming His name, and within His name is 'I am a God who forgives and has everlasting patience'. So Moses said, "See, I told You. That is Your name. I am claiming that." And God promised, "I will go with You and I will keep the covenant."

That's the message I preached in Toronto. (Now, if there is any place where the fire can fall, it is Toronto. You can sneeze and lay out half the people. So I got to the end and said, "Lord, release Your glory;" and waited for the fireworks. Well, there was a little pause and people started shaking. Then, people all over the place started lying down on the floor. Now, the Toronto church has a huge front area that is empty, plus adjoining aisles. Pretty soon, over 1000 people were lying down everywhere, and it got really quiet. I thought, "I have put people to sleep with my sermons before but I have never been this effective!" So I finally just sat down next to John Arnott and said, "Okay John, I think I'm done," and he just looked at me and didn't even say anything; so I just sat there for 15 or 20 minutes with nothing going on. You just can't do that in church. You have to have something going on.

So I went home and prayed, "Lord, every other time I have done this Your fire has come, and the anointing has come, and we've prayed for people and they'd go flying, and we'd just have a wonderful time. What is this?"

Some time later, I was impacted by a prophecy I received that was dated January 4, 2002, and titled, "2002 A Year of Rest, Preparation and Breakthrough": 2002 will begin the entering of the Sabbath rest. The true lordship of Christ and His resurrection glory is about to be revealed in a most profound manner to those who have pursued intimacy with Him. We now understand that Christ Himself is our Sabbath, and we are to labor to enter into the fullness of His presence and rest. There is a great wave of healing and deliverance coming to the Church for the purpose of healing the wounded body of Christ, releasing the harvest. One problem that will rise is that religious people will become very angry and embittered toward those who are pursuing Him in rest. In entering His rest there will be unlimited provision, unlimited love and intimacy, unlimited authority, and unlimited opportunity. We will begin to see Him and the beauty of His riches, His resurrection glory and holiness; and no longer just as He is presented in the gospels in poverty as the lowly servant. The shekinah cloud of His presence will be seen resting in places and geographical regions around the world. This will prepare us to come into intimate oneness with Him and His purpose and to be trusted with greater anointing, authority, and responsibility.

Previously, I had been in the San Jose area praying for deliverance with a lady. There were five of us present; as I began, out of my mouth came these words, "Now, you need to understand, I did not plan to say these things. You understand this don't you? Lord, take us to the fourth dimension for this deliverance." All of a sudden, it was like we were in an elevator and we started going up. The power of God hit the woman and she started shaking, so we all just sat there while the Lord did deliverance on her. I wasn't needed any more, so I was looking around trying to decide what I was supposed to do and had the thought, "Paul, try to worry about something right now."

I must tell you that I could have received a gold medal for worry in my life. I was a great worrier—not warrior—worrier. I could worry with the best of them. I'm sure I could surpass you at any level, and I had some big things to worry about too; you know you're alive if you have things to worry about.

So there I was, trying to worry but couldn't! I thought, "What is this place?" and said to the other four people, "Try to worry right now." They started laughing and said, "We can't worry." We had gone to another place.

I want you to follow me now. The Bible says we are seated with Christ in heavenly places, not in a place. The scientific and mathematical names for those places are dimensions. That is biblical, but we are not there all the time. Positionally we should be, but in our soul and our spirit we are not always there...

...And God says to us, "Now make every effort to enter into the rest." [2] So, there is one thing we need to work at friends, and this is it—we need to work at entering His rest. Why?

I heard Heidi Baker speak, and she helped me understand this because she has learned to enter into the rest; she lives there. Everything happens in His rest. It's where ideas come; it's where strategies

---

[2] Matthew 11:28-29; Hebrews 4:1, Hebrews 4:9

come. it's where warfare takes place; it's where ministries are birthed. It's in His presence, in His rest where I no longer need to plan and scheme. I do not need to start a media ministry. I do not need to try to raise money for buildings. I don't really need to do anything except go into His rest and let Him do it. It's a new way of doing church...

...I don't care whether you are a businessman or a minister, it works. There are going to be new kinds of board meetings in which an entire board will to enter into His rest and let Him speak. And they will say, "Oh my goodness, what a wonderful idea," but they will no longer claim the ideas as their own.

Isaiah says, "Lord all that I have done You have accomplished for me."[3] Do you understand that every good thought, every good thing that you do is His idea? He just lets us look good while He's doing it.

There are two ways that you know that you have entered His rest. One is that it is impossible to worry, and the second is that you cannot be jealous of anyone else's gifts...

...Enjoy His place of rest. It is the Holy of Holies, the tent of meeting, Mount Zion, the secret place, the place of intimacy, the shelter of the Most High, the tent of His presence, the mountain of the Lord,

---

[3] Isaiah 26:12

the bedchamber, God's bosom, a place of waiting. It is the higher ground.

The closer we get to the Day of the Lord, the more intense the battle will become; the enemy will pull out every weapon in his arsenal to prevent Jesus' second coming, the worst of which is fear. It is more important than ever before to enter the rest of the Lord.

CHAPTER TWO:
FEAR & ITS BYPRODUCTS

"Just wait until your father gets home!" While I don't remember what my mother was angry with me about, I do remember the exact location and time of day. She had taken us into town to shop, and my brother and I had been playing in the town square. Whatever the infraction, it was early in the day, and long hours loomed ahead until our dad got home from work; so what began as a fun outing suddenly became a day of dread. Needless fear, as it turned out, because by the time he walked in the door that evening, Mom had apparently forgotten all about her earlier threat. Whew!

I'm certain that any fear of my father's expected punishment pales in comparison to that of Adam and Eve in the Garden of Eden:

> *So when the woman saw that the tree was good for food, and that it was a delight to the eyes, and that the tree was to be desired to make one wise, she took of its fruit and ate, and she also gave some to her husband who was with her, and he ate. Then the eyes of both were opened, and they knew that they were naked. And they sewed fig leaves together and made themselves loincloths. And they heard the sound of the Lord God walking in the garden in the cool of the day, and the man and his wife hid themselves from the presence of the Lord God among the*

trees of the garden. But the Lord God called to the man and said to him, "Where are you? And he said, "I heard the sound of you in the garden, and I was afraid, because I was naked, and I hid myself." [1]

It's a well-known Bible story, so familiar that regardless of how many times it's been repeated, we might have missed one of its most important points. The very first experiential consequence of that first sin was fear. When God asked, "Where are you?" Adam answered, "I was afraid." The new knowledge they had just received didn't turn out to be quite the wonderful thing that the serpent had promised. Can you imagine their distress as Adam and Eve quickly sewed fig leaves into clothing, frantically trying to hide from the wrath they now expected from their Father? What a shock! With a taste of fruit, life had suddenly shifted from glorious contentment to fearful anxiety; and that fear introduced four previously un-familiar concepts — lack, want, need and expect. Now, instead of resting in the bounty of God's earthly garden and basking in His presence, they now lacked, wanted and desperately needed a covering for their nakedness. Even worse, they expected punishment instead of God's loving kindness. Fear and its byproducts were born that day.

We define fear as an emotion that is induced by a perceived danger or threat, which causes physiological changes and, ultimately, behavioral changes such as fleeing, hiding, or

---

[1] Genesis 3:6-10

freezing from perceived traumatic events.[2] Only recently did we fully realize that fear was also the first-fruit of sin, and Paul began wondering if it might be a root to all psychological disorders. He spoke with two psychologists, both of whom agreed that while not scientifically provable, it is certainly possible. It appears that fear is a very strong primordial emotion that may lie at the root of many other issues. Medical professionals, myself included, have often observed instances in which fear has escalated our patients' suffering.

Dr Earl Henslin,[3] a Christian psychologist, is an expert in reading SPECT brain imaging scans, identifying physical evidence of psychological problems. He shared with Paul:

> During the last eight-to-ten years, everyone has an overactive place in the basal ganglia. This is the anxiety thermostat in the brain. It is the area of the brain where we talk about fear; it influences muscles, head aches (including migraines) and gastrointestinal problems; it is the area of panic attacks and fear. When it gets over-activated, it de-stabilizes the whole brain, which then opens itself up to attacks from evil. Because of this, it affects us so that we do not have good boundaries.

Dr. Henslin has reported that scans performed after a person practices Christian meditation (staying in the presence of the Holy Spirit while focusing on Father, Son

---

[2] en.wikipedia.org/wiki/Fear
[3] drhenslin.com

and Holy Spirit; NOT simply keeping an open mind) indicates a decrease in agitation when compared to a baseline scan.

When sin entered into human experience, fear became the constant result of disobedience to God's commandments, and fear still occurs when we don't obey Him. Just as in the Garden, we have often believed that He would become vindictive in His anger toward us:

> *Your life shall hang in doubt before you. Night and day you shall be in dread and have no assurance of your life. In the morning you shall say, 'If only it were evening!' and at evening you shall say, 'If only it were morning!' because of the dread that your heart shall feel, and the sights that your eyes shall see."* [4]

I imagine all of us have felt like that on occasion. Perhaps we have become bound up by fear over what might happen next; waiting for the next shoe to drop so to speak, unwittingly falling into an attitude akin to Murphy's Law and expecting that anything that can go wrong will go wrong. Getting back to Adam and Eve; clearly they were afraid of God's reaction, but what happened? He immediately:[5]

- Cursed the serpent
- Announced His redemptive plan

---

[4] Deuteronomy 28:66–67
[5] Genesis 3:14-24

- Informed them that life was going to become very hard; but then turned right around and made garments of skins for them, evidence of Hos continuing loving kindness
- Evicted them from the garden and blocked access to the Tree of Life so they would not have to live forever in their fallen state, preparing a way for them to be saved from eternal destruction

Sadly, while Adam and Eve suddenly had knowledge of good and evil, they did not yet comprehend the surety of God's enduring love:

> *There is no fear in love, but perfect love casts out fear. For fear has to do with punishment, and whoever fears has not been perfected in love.*[6]

God's wrath definitely is something to fear, but only if one rejects Him:

> *Know therefore that the Lord your God is God, the faithful God who keeps covenant and steadfast love with those who love him and keep his commandments, to a thousand generations, and repays to their face those who hate him, by destroying them. He will not be slack with one who hates him. He will repay him to his face.*[7]

---

[6] 1 John 4:18
[7] Deuteronomy 7:9-10

It is a terrifying thing to fall into the hands of the living God.[8]

The truth is that God's love for us knows no bounds:

But you, O Lord, are a God merciful and gracious, slow to anger and abounding in steadfast love and faithfulness.[9]

Give thanks to the God of heaven, for his steadfast love endures forever.[10]

For God so loved the world that he gave his only Son, that whoever believes in him should not perish but have eternal life. For God did not send his Son into the world to condemn the world, but in order that the world might be saved through him.[11]

God shows his love for us in that while we were still sinners, Christ died for us.[12]

But God, being rich in mercy, because of the great love with which he loved us, even when we were dead in our trespasses, made us alive together with Christ — by grace you have been saved — and raised us up with him and seated us with him in the heavenly places in Christ Jesus, so that in the coming ages he might show the

---

[8] Hebrews 10:31
[9] Psalm 86:15
[10] Psalm 136:26
[11] John 3:16-17
[12] Romans 5:8

> *immeasurable riches of his grace in kindness toward us in Christ Jesus.*[13]

Wonderful promises, but some may still argue that the Bible talks a lot about the fear of the Lord. Our response is that yes, it does, but keep in mind that the enemy's version of fearing God is a scare tactic that is nothing but a very deceptive imitation, a counterfeit, of the righteous-and-holy fear of the Lord:

> *...the fear of the Lord is clean, enduring forever...*[14]

This holy fear of the Lord is meant to be an expression of awe and reverence for God. It is also one of the seven Spirits of the Lord.[15]

Contrast that with the enemy's version of fear, which has to do with a state of feeling great distress, and deep concern of pain or unfavorable circumstance. [16] Sadly, this is what Adam, Eve and every person since has fallen prey to; but we do not have to live there, for the truth in God's own words is:

---

[13] Ephesians 2:4-7
[14] Psalm 19:9a
[15] Isaiah 11:2
[16] Swanson, J. (1997). *Dictionary of Biblical Languages with Semantic Domains : Hebrew (Old Testament)* (electronic ed.). Oak Harbor: Logos Research Systems, Inc.

...fear not, for I am with you; be not dismayed, for I am your God; I will strengthen you, I will help you, I will uphold you with my righteous right hand.[17]

Fearful expectations, as simple as my own worry over what might happen when Dad got home, or as life-shattering as that of Adam and Eve when they expected God's wrath, are destructive. Fear seems to be the lowest common denominator of want, need, lack and expect; and just as our ancient parents earnestly desired clothing to cover their nakedness and expected punishment, so do we often focus on the things we want, even while fearing that something will go wrong and we won't be able to obtain them. That root of doubt and unbelief is really fear that God will not do what He says He will do; therefore, He cannot be trusted to fulfill His promises.

---

[17] Isaiah 41:10

CHAPTER THREE:
THE ROOT OF DESIRE

Want, need and lack; three words that are so closely aligned as to be synonymous and all-too-familiar in everyday life. They flow together in a vicious cycle that produces false expectations. A friend recently offered her perspective, one that I find to be very wise:

> One of the saddest things to me are cases when a Christian doesn't know how to tell the difference between a want and a need. That leads to countless problems, especially financial ones. If you get need mixed up with want you'll definitely experience lack eventually. Then, after suffering lack, if there is no surrender to God, a growing expectation will develop for Him or for other people to bail them out. After all, it couldn't be their fault. Sometimes a well-meaning friend or family member may try to help, too often starting a horrible cycle of enabling, not only for current but also future crises. It's a very, very sad thing to watch; it is hard to watch a loved one or friend implode because they have come to expect their wants and needs to be met so they will have no lack. One thing leads to another, spiraling down a rabbit hole.

Let's go back to our old friends, Adam and Eve, and examine how their 'spiral down the rabbit hole' set the stage for the rest of humanity down through succeeding generations. From the very first moment, every need was provided by God and it was very good:

> *So God created man in his own image, in the image of God he created him; male and female he created them. And God blessed them. And God said to them, "Be fruitful and multiply and fill the earth and subdue it, and have dominion over the fish of the sea and over the birds of the heavens and over every living thing that moves on the earth." And God said, "Behold, I have given you every plant yielding seed that is on the face of all the earth, and every tree with seed in its fruit. You shall have them for food. And to every beast of the earth and to every bird of the heavens and to everything that creeps on the earth, everything that has the breath of life, I have given every green plant for food." And it was so. And God saw everything that he had made, and behold, it was very good. And there was evening and there was morning, the sixth day.[1]*

Their home Eden, a lush garden that we might think of as akin to Shangri-La, a mythical paradise that's too good to be true. But it was true; there was just one thing in all of God's creation that was not allowed:

> *And out of the ground the Lord God made to spring up every tree that is pleasant to the sight and good for food. The tree of life was in the midst of the garden, and the*

---

[1] Genesis 1:27-31

> *tree of the knowledge of good and evil. A river flowed out of Eden to water the garden, and there it divided and became four rivers…The Lord God took the man and put him in the garden of Eden to work it and keep it. And the Lord God commanded the man, saying, "You may surely eat of every tree of the garden, but of the tree of the knowledge of good and evil you shall not eat, for in the day that you eat of it you shall surely die."*[2]

Our ancient ancestors had everything except the fruit of one tree; they didn't even have to water the garden! But it wasn't enough, and their want, or desire, for that luscious-looking fruit morphed into something the enemy convinced them they needed to truly be like God. Never mind the fact that they had been created in His image and enjoyed walking and talking with Him each day in their extraordinary home. Satan convinced them that God was holding back something good, and the forbidden fruit would fill the lack in their lives. Unfortunately for them and for us, they fell right down into the very rabbit hole that has become commonplace in our own lives.

As we seek after the things of God, there are definitely righteous aspects of want, need, lack and expect; but for now we'll examine the fallout of that first sin. We want that which we don't have and such want is nothing less than covetousness, which is expressly prohibited in God's ten commandments.[3] Biblical study indicates:

---

[2] Genesis 2:9-10, 15-17
[3] Exodus 20:17

Wanting and Desiring. The expression "desire" or "inordinate longing" is reflected in the OT primarily by the roots *'wh* and *hmd*... The words *'wh* and *hmd* are synonymous and often appear in parallelism (Gen 3:6) [4]

Genesis 3:6 takes us back to Eden, the origin of our want:

So when the woman saw that the tree was good for food, and that it was a delight to the eyes, and that the tree was to be desired to make one wise, she took of its fruit and ate, and she also gave some to her husband who was with her, and he ate.

As want has escalated throughout history, God's Word has made it clear that it is often caused by hastiness, greed, sloth, debauchery, reckless living and self-centeredness:

Desire without knowledge is not good, and whoever makes haste with his feet misses his way. [5]

The plans of the diligent lead surely to abundance, but everyone who is hasty comes only to poverty. [6]

For the wicked boasts of the desires of his soul, and the one greedy for gain curses and renounces the LORD. [7]

---

[4] Schunck, K.-D. (1992). Wanting and Desiring. In D. N. Freedman (Ed.), P. R. Callaway (Trans.), *The Anchor Yale Bible Dictionary* (Vol. 6, p. 866). New York: Doubleday.
[5] Proverbs 19:2
[6] Proverbs 21:5
[7] Psalm 10:3

Whoever oppresses the poor to increase his own wealth, or gives to the rich, will only come to poverty.[8]

I passed by the field of a sluggard, by the vineyard of a man lacking sense,[9]

Then they brought in the golden vessels that had been taken out of the temple, the house of God in Jerusalem, and the king and his lords, his wives, and his concubines drank from them. They drank wine and praised the gods of gold and silver, bronze, iron, wood, and stone. Immediately the fingers of a human hand appeared and wrote on the plaster of the wall of the king's palace... TEKEL, you have been weighed in the balances and found wanting.[10]

Not many days later, the younger son gathered all he had and took a journey into a far country, and there he squandered his property in reckless living. And when he had spent everything, a severe famine arose in that country, and he began to be in need.[11]

But if you have bitter jealousy and selfish ambition in your hearts, do not boast and be false to the truth. This is not the wisdom that comes down from above, but is earthly, unspiritual, demonic. For where jealousy and

---

[8] Proverbs 22:16
[9] Proverbs 24:30-34
[10] Daniel 5:3-5, 27
[11] Luke 15:13-14

selfish ambition exist, there will be disorder and every vile practice.[12]

Tragically, like Adam and Eve, we have too-often believed the enemy's lie that God is holding back that which is good and ended up blaming Him for our perceived lack. We forget the truth:

For the LORD is good; his steadfast love endures forever, and his faithfulness to all generations.[13]

God is not the one responsible for our plight![14] Rather, He stands ready to help at every turn:

And my God will supply every need of yours according to his riches in glory in Christ Jesus.[15]

… your Father knows what you need before you ask him.[16]

For all the nations of the world seek after these things, and your Father knows that you need them. Instead, seek his kingdom, and these things will be added to you.[17]

For we do not have a high priest who is unable to sympathize with our weaknesses, but one who in every

---

[12] James 3:13-16
[13] Psalm 100:5
[14] God's steadfast goodness and love is discussed extensively in *Exploring Heavenly Places, Volume 11: This Present Battle* or at aslansplace.com/the-answer-to-the-question/
[15] Philippians 4:19
[16] Matthew 6:8b
[17] Luke 12:30–31

respect has been tempted as we are, yet without sin. Let us then with confidence draw near to the throne of grace, that we may receive mercy and find grace to help in time of need.[18]

How tragic that we have believed the enemy's lie that God does not have our best interests at heart, mistrusting Him because we haven't learned to abide in the love He graciously offers.[19] My wise friend also had a bit to say about that:

> Those who have never learned to tell the difference between the Lord speaking and their own mind speaking get mixed up and make unwise decisions. In both want and need, the accompanying lack may result from not abiding in Christ. For me, abiding is the door that leads to the beginning of wisdom, abundance, and more. He's given us His righteousness because He loves us and wants us to be overcomers.

Amen! His promised love answers every want, need and lack we experience, and when we abide in it our expectations are transformed into a hope that does not disappoint.[20]

---

[18] Hebrews 4:14–16
[19] John 15:9-11
[20] Romans 5:5

CHAPTER FOUR:
WANT

We live in a goal-setting society, and that's not necessarily a bad thing unless our goals are based on our wants rather than on what God wants for us. I fell into that trap while still a teenager. Saved at eight years old and raised in a Christian home, I loved God and knew that He had placed a call upon my life. I didn't know for sure what that would eventually look like, but assumed that if I could achieve just three goals that I was passionate about, life would be perfect; I would be happy and serve God; He would be happy about my commitment. So, I headed off to begin fulfilling my dreams two weeks after high school graduation, all set to achieve my goals to become a registered nurse, get married and have a baby. All three quests were fraught with obstacles, but had finally been accomplished by the time I was thirty. So why did I still feel so empty?

I will be forever grateful (in the order the goals were accomplished) for my nursing career, my husband and my son; each is a wonderful gift from God, but seeking them first was a mistake. I should have heeded the oh-so-familiar and cherished words of Jesus:

> *Seek first the kingdom of God and his righteousness, and all these things will be added to you.*[1]

How much more peaceful might my life have been if I had been mature enough as a Christian to follow the example of Paul the Apostle:

> *Brothers, I do not consider that I have made it my own. But one thing I do: forgetting what lies behind and straining forward to what lies ahead, I press on toward the goal for the prize of the upward call of God in Christ Jesus.*[2]

How often God's people have fallen into the trap of thinking they know what's best for them. A word received in 2006 reminded us of Israel's demand for a king so they could be like everybody else. It was an unworthy goal:

> I feel that the Lord would say, "We are like the Old Testament people who wanted kings. They always wanted Sauls to reign and rule over them. My people still look for Sauls; they exalt them, cling to them like little gods. Do you know what it does to My heart as you bow down at their feet? It breaks my heart to see them running after Sauls and not after Me. I would open up a banquet table for you if you run after Me. Why won't you run to Me? I have everything you would ever need or want. Harken to My heart and My voice; I will give Saul a

---

[1] Matthew 6:33
[2] Philippians 3:13-14

chance to repent, but then a hammer will come to destroy all that Saul has built. The earth has only seen Sauls, but My kingdom is coming; it will be through small ministries that stay small in their own eyes, and not large ministries. There is a wave that's going to come through this land. It is not a water wave; it is a wave of fire. To some it will be an answer to prayer, and ministries will be born; there will be revitalization. But to others it will be devastation."

God's displeasure was echoed through the prophet, Samuel:

But the thing displeased Samuel when they said, "Give us a king to judge us." And Samuel prayed to the Lord. And the Lord said to Samuel, "Obey the voice of the people in all that they say to you, for they have not rejected you, but they have rejected me from being king over them. According to all the deeds that they have done, from the day I brought them up out of Egypt even to this day, forsaking me and serving other gods, so they are also doing to you. Now then, obey their voice; only you shall solemnly warn them and show them the ways of the king who shall reign over them." [3]

Fast-forward back to the present and consider a 2016 survey that explored a key question, "If you could say in one word what you want more of in life, what would that be?" Among

---

[3] 1 Samuel 8:6-9

771 respondents, the eight things mentioned most frequently were happiness, money, freedom, peace, joy, balance, fulfillment and confidence.[4]

An internet search investigating how to best achieve those wants included goal-setting in almost every article I read. There was even one statement from a goal-setting coach, declaring that it is more than just practical—it's a prerequisite for happiness. No, there is a much better way, and a condensed review of prophetic words we have received at Aslan's Place, interspersed with associated scriptures, offers much wiser guidance.

> 2005: There is tension between what we want and what He wants… He wants to nurture us so we can go deeper into His wells; He wants us to go deeper, deeper, deeper, deeper; treasures are there; the enemy does not like it. He wants surrendered hearts.

> *The sacrifices of God are a broken spirit, A broken and a contrite heart — These, O God, You will not despise.*[5]

> 2008: You must come up higher. Let Me take you higher… He wants to give you a new heart, a new mind. This is the time of crossing over. Do not be afraid to get wet. This is the time to play. The Lord has much for us. There is a river to play in.

---

[4] forbes.com/sites/kathycaprino/2016/05/24/the-top-8-things-people-desperately-desire-but-cant-seem-to-attain/#3a99c477086c
[5] Psalm 51:17

THE MYSTERY OF THE ANCIENT PATHS

And I will give you a new heart, and a new spirit I will put within you. And I will remove the heart of stone from your flesh and give you a heart of flesh.[6]

2009: To go higher you have to go lower. You have to live with dissatisfaction. You cannot be satisfied with the present for you must always want to know more.

My people are destroyed for lack of knowledge; because you have rejected knowledge, I reject you from being a priest to me. And since you have forgotten the law of your God, I also will forget your children.[7]

The fear of the LORD is the beginning of knowledge; fools despise wisdom and instruction.[8]

Take my instruction instead of silver, and knowledge rather than choice gold, for wisdom is better than jewels, and all that you may desire cannot compare with her.[9]

Like newborn infants, long for the pure spiritual milk, that by it you may grow up into salvation – if indeed you have tasted that the Lord is good.[10]

2009: This may look serious to you, but it will be fun, fun, fun. I am a God who loves fun, but I can be serious also. I want you to ride with Me. For I

---

[6] Ezekiel 36:26
[7] Hosea 4:6
[8] Proverbs 1:7
[9] Proverbs 8:10–11
[10] 1 Peter 2:1–3

am taking you to new places, new depths; fly with Me, come with Me. There are treasures down here for each one of you. I want you to dare to dream. There is much I want to give you; so much I want to give you.

If you then, who are evil, know how to give good gifts to your children, how much more will your Father who is in heaven give good things to those who ask him![11]

2010: Do as I say, and not what you want. Do My will; hear My voice. I am crying in the wilderness. Listen to My voice. Obedience is the key. Tell My people to come in; I love them.

For this is the love of God, that we keep his commandments. And his commandments are not burdensome.[12]

2010: The Lord wants us to have the heart of a child, to play in the garden. Totally and absolutely trust that He has a plan and wants us to prosper. Develop that child-like faith. The battle belongs to the Lord. No worry at all. Receive the heart of a child.

Jesus said, "Let the little children come to me and do not hinder them, for to such belongs the kingdom of heaven."[13]

---

[11] Matthew 7:11
[12] 1 John 5:3
[13] Matthew 19:14

2012: I call for cleansing, cleansing of the land. I will root up and I will establish. I will gather you under My wings; I will protect you. You need not fear. I tell you, get rid of the leaven, the small foxes that spoil the vine. I want to show you My face. I want to breathe new life into you. I want to! I want to! Will you let Me? Will you draw near to Me? Will you put down what is in your hand and let Me fill you? I will direct your path and I will make this land sing. My victory is sure and it is at hand. I am angered; I say that enough is enough; I will tolerate no more. It is time to square your shoulders and stand up straight for victory is at hand.

He who dwells in the shelter of the Most High will abide in the shadow of the Almighty. I will say to the Lord, "My refuge and my fortress, my God, in whom I trust." For he will deliver you from the snare of the fowler and from the deadly pestilence. He will cover you with his pinions, and under his wings you will find refuge; his faithfulness is a shield and buckler.[14]

O my dove, in the clefts of the rock, in the crannies of the cliff, let me see your face, let me hear your voice, for your voice is sweet, and your face is lovely. Catch the foxes for us, the little foxes that spoil the vineyards, for our vineyards are in blossom.[15]

---

[14] Psalm 91:1-4
[15] Song of Solomon 2:14-15

Trust in the Lord with all your heart, and do not lean on your own understanding. In all your ways acknowledge him, and he will make straight your paths.[16]

June 29, 2013: Paul wrote, "During coaching today the Lord revealed a corrupted gate and doors. The Lord showed that it was a wall of jealousy. This is the jealousy of God, where people want to be God and do what they want to do rather than doing what He wants to do.

Take care, lest you forget the covenant of the Lord your God, which he made with you, and make a carved image, the form of anything that the Lord your God has forbidden you. For the Lord your God is a consuming fire, a jealous God.[17]

2016: There is so much that I have for you beyond what you ask and imagine. The heavens are full with answers; the heavens are full of your dreams. You have only to reach out to Me. My children want to fulfill their own dreams and desires while I stand at the door knocking, but not just for salvation. Let Me be who I am. Look at the universe. What is bigger than that? Man is still trying to get to the edge, but you will never reach the end of Me. Come with Me; I want to show you. Come with me; I long for someone to come with Me. I created you for companionship. All I have is yours; I want to watch

---

[16] Proverbs 3:5-6
[17] Deuteronomy 4:23-24

your faces in complete joy and wonder, like you look at your own children.

Father, I desire that they also, whom you have given me, may be with me where I am, to see my glory that you have given me because you loved me before the foundation of the world. O righteous Father, even though the world does not know you, I know you, and these know that you have sent me. I made known to them your name, and I will continue to make it known, that the love with which you have loved me may be in them, and I in them." [18]

The first sentence of that first word from 2005 sums it all up; there is tension between what we want and what He wants. Like toddlers insisting, "Me do it!" we try to fulfill of our own wants. Meanwhile, God stands there patiently like any loving parent would do, allowing us to learn, often the hard way! He waits to lend a hand and grant our hearts' desires if we will only accept His help. We would do well to remember just how much He wants to provide for us, as King David expressed so eloquently:

The Lord is my shepherd; I shall not want. He makes me lie down in green pastures. He leads me beside still waters. He restores my soul. He leads me in paths of righteousness for his name's sake. Even though I walk through the valley of the shadow of death, I will fear no evil, for you are with me; your rod and your staff, they comfort me. You prepare a table before me in the presence

---

[18] John 17:24-26

of my enemies; you anoint my head with oil; my cup overflows. Surely goodness and mercy shall follow me all the days of my life, and I shall dwell in the house of the Lord forever.[19]

---

[19] Psalm 23

CHAPTER FIVE:
THREE PERSPECTIVES OF WANT

Perspective is a particular way of considering something. Artists' works, for example, vary in a multitude of ways depending on the artist's vision, media, style, etc. The finished work of a diverse group of artists viewing the same scene could result in paintings, sculptures, music, dance or poetry. It pretty-much boils down to what one wants to achieve with the finished work. With that in mind, it might be wise to consider three important perspectives of want to gain greater understanding.

God's Perspective:
In the beginning, God created the heavens and the earth,[1] so let's begin there with His perspective. What does He appear to want most? Surprisingly enough, it is to have a relationship with mankind. We are the only beings created in His image, and it was for us that He created the world in the first place. A perfect relationship between God and man existed within a perfect environment before that pesky original sin ruined it all. We are the ones for whom He sent His Son to secure redemption by dying in our place, and destroying the curse of death for all who would accept His sacrifice. Certainly, the Father didn't want Jesus to die, but He did it out of of His love for us; He did it because He wants us that desperately:

---

[1] Genesis 1:1

For one will scarcely die for a righteous person – though perhaps for a good person one would dare even to die – but God shows his love for us in that while we were still sinners, Christ died for us. Since, therefore, we have now been justified by his blood, much more shall we be saved by him from the wrath of God. For if while we were enemies we were reconciled to God by the death of his Son, much more, now that we are reconciled, shall we be saved by his life.[2]

For I desire steadfast love and not sacrifice, the knowledge of God rather than burnt offerings.[3]

Go and learn what this means: 'I desire mercy, and not sacrifice.' For I came not to call the righteous, but sinners."[4]

Father, I desire that they also, whom you have given me, may be with me where I am, to see my glory that you have given me because you loved me before the foundation of the world.[5]

Satan's Perspective:

The previous discussion regarding Satan's deception of Adam and Eve clearly illustrates that the total destruction of God's beloved mankind tops his list of wants. The devil's depravity is clear, and his appetite is always for evil:

---

[2] Romans 5:7-10
[3] Hosea 6:6
[4] Matthew 9:13
[5] John 17:24

Be sober-minded; be watchful. Your adversary the devil prowls around like a roaring lion, seeking someone to devour.[6]

You are of your father the devil, and your will is to do your father's desires. He was a murderer from the beginning, and does not stand in the truth, because there is no truth in him. When he lies, he speaks out of his own character, for he is a liar and the father of lies.[7]

I imagine the enemy's biggest desire throughout time has been to do everything in his power to corrupt God's agenda; his hatred of our Lord knows no bounds. First, he tried to steal God's beloved mankind away forever by manipulating them into trading eternal life for certain death. Then, throughout the Old Testament he tormented God's people on every hand, with Job being an early example:

And the Lord said to Satan, "Have you considered my servant Job, that there is none like him on the earth, a blameless and upright man, who fears God and turns away from evil?"[9] Then Satan answered the Lord and said, "Does Job fear God for no reason? Have you not put a hedge around him and his house and all that he has, on every side? You have blessed the work of his hands, and his possessions have increased in the land. But stretch

---

[6] 1 Peter 5:8
[7] John 8:44

out your hand and touch all that he has, and he will curse you to your face." [8]

But then Jesus came along and Satan knew very well who He was; so the next trick in his bag was to try to convince the Son of Man to sin, just like every other human being since Eden had done. After all, only a sinless Jesus could save His creation:

And he was in the wilderness forty days, being tempted by Satan. And he was with the wild animals, and the angels were ministering to him. [9]

And Jesus answered him, "It is said, 'You shall not put the Lord your God to the test.'" And when the devil had ended every temptation, he departed from him until an opportune time. [10]

That didn't work out so well, so the next thing the enemy tried was to get Jesus killed. We all know how badly that backfired, when our Savior willingly died and then proceeded to take back that which Satan had stolen:

During supper, when the devil had already put it into the heart of Judas Iscariot, Simon's son, to betray him... [11]

"Therefore My Father loves Me, because I lay down My life that I may take it again. No one takes it from Me, but

---

[8] Job 1:8-11
[9] Mark 1:13
[10] Luke 4:12-13
[11] John 13:2

48

I lay it down of Myself. I have power to lay it down, and I have power to take it again. This command I have received from My Father." [12]

When I saw him, I fell at his feet as though dead. But he laid his right hand on me, saying, "Fear not, I am the first and the last, and the living one. I died, and behold I am alive forevermore, and I have the keys of Death and Hades.[13]

Oops — another big backfire on another evil plan! So, the next thing on the devil's list of wants became to make the lives of people so difficult that they would either refuse to accept Jesus or render them helpless to further God's kingdom if they did receive Him. Blatantly evil, his attacks are unfortunately effective all too often. He disguises himself so as to appear good, and actively fights against our faith:

For such men are false apostles, deceitful workmen, disguising themselves as apostles of Christ. And no wonder, for even Satan disguises himself as an angel of light.[14]

For we do not wrestle against flesh and blood, but against the rulers, against the authorities, against the cosmic

---

[12] John 10:17-18
[13] Revelation 1:17-18
[14] 2 Corinthians 11:13-14

powers over this present darkness, against the spiritual forces of evil in the heavenly places.[15]

As he did with Job, the devil often torments us with infirmity and loss; he pulls out all the stops trying to destroy us:

The field is the world, and the good seed is the sons of the kingdom. The weeds are the sons of the evil one, and the enemy who sowed them is the devil.[16]

Do not love the world or the things in the world. If anyone loves the world, the love of the Father is not in him. For all that is in the world – the desires of the flesh and the desires of the eyes and pride of life – is not from the Father but is from the world.[17]

Evidence of the enemy's persecution of God's people flows throughout the Old and New Testaments, and it is obvious in modern-day life as we witness ever-increasing persecution of the Church, with martyrdom becoming more and more common in many areas of the world:

Blessed are you when others revile you and persecute you and utter all kinds of evil against you falsely on my account. Rejoice and be glad, for your reward is great in

---

[15] Ephesians 6:12
[16] Matthew 13:38-39
[17] 1 John 2:15-16

heaven, for so they persecuted the prophets who were before you.[18]

Do not fear what you are about to suffer. Behold, the devil is about to throw some of you into prison, that you may be tested, and for ten days you will have tribulation. Be faithful unto death, and I will give you the crown of life.[19]

Enough of Satan's agenda to wreak havoc in order to fulfill his desires; let's move on.

Mankind's Perspective:

God created us with free will, the gift of choice; but He wants us to choose wisely. The foundation of His throne is righteousness and justice, so it only makes sense that our decisions should align with His will:

So Jesus answered them, "My teaching is not mine, but his who sent me. If anyone's will is to do God's will, he will know whether the teaching is from God or whether I am speaking on my own authority.[20]

For you were called to freedom, brothers. Only do not use your freedom as an opportunity for the flesh, but through love serve one another. For the whole law is fulfilled in one word: "You shall love your neighbor as yourself."… For the desires of the flesh are against the Spirit, and the desires of the Spirit are against the flesh, for these are

---

[18] Matthew 5:11-12
[19] Revelation 2:10
[20] John 7:17

opposed to each other, to keep you from doing the things you want to do.[21]

God's perspective is clear; Satan's perspective is clear; our perspective is a choice between the two. Tremendous blessings are associated with God's way; but terrible consequences come with the enemy's way; the contrast is literally life or death:

For as by the one man's [Adam's] disobedience the many were made sinners, so by the one man's [Christ's] obedience the many will be made righteous.[22]

For as in Adam all die, so also in Christ shall all be made alive.[23]

Our choice of perspective should be clear, and we agree with Joshua's decision:

Now therefore fear the Lord and serve him in sincerity and in faithfulness. Put away the gods that your fathers served beyond the River and in Egypt, and serve the Lord. And if it is evil in your eyes to serve the Lord, choose this day whom you will serve, whether the gods your fathers served in the region beyond the River, or the gods of the Amorites in whose land you dwell. But as for me and my house, we will serve the Lord.[24]

---

[21] Galatians 5:13-14, 17
[22] Romans 5:19
[23] 1 Corinthians 15:22
[24] Joshua 24:14-15

Chapter Six:
NEED

"Mommy, I neeeed it; pleeese," implored my young son. He was on his knees with hands folded and held up as if in prayer, and an irresistible, pleading-but-grinning look on his face as I unloaded my groceries onto the checkout counter. I couldn't help laughing and relented, "Yes, this time, but that will only work once!" The toy he needed so badly was a piece of junk that he would buy with his own money; one that I'd said no to repeatedly, knowing it would be a total waste of his hard-earned ten dollars. He was so happy to get what he wanted; but his joy lasted for all of about 10 minutes after it was out of the package because it broke and could not be fixed.

How often have we been like that, convinced we needed something so badly that we made unwise decisions in order to satisfy perceived needs? If you're like me the answer is probably too often. You see, a need isn't that perfect car, home, boat, vacation or expensive trinket that digs the hole of debt deeper and deeper. It isn't that perfect job for which relationships have to be sacrificed. It isn't wealth, power or fame; and it isn't even to happiness, contrary to popular thought. Rather, a need is something that is necessary for a safe, stable and healthy life; needs encompass such things as air, water, food and shelter. Additionally, people have needs of a social or societal nature, such as the human need to socialize or belong to a family unit or group.[1]

This is about where some might interject an objection, "What about Maslow's hierarchy of needs?" [2] Good question, and our answer is that the farther one progresses in his theory, going beyond basic physiologic needs into those having to do with psychological and self-fulfillment needs, the more one enters into dependence on self and others rather than on God.

> *Now as the king of Israel was passing by on the wall, a woman cried out to him, saying, "Help, my lord, O king!" And he said, "If the Lord will not help you, how shall I help you?" [3]*

While Maslow does legitimately identify safety, security and relationships as important needs, we must always be careful to remember that those are all available in God, and He is much more capable of supplying them than we are:

> *Then the Lord God said, "It is not good that the man should be alone; I will make him a helper fit for[him.[4]*

> *He who dwells in the shelter of the Most High will abide in the shadow of the Almighty. I will say to the Lord, "My refuge and my fortress, my God, in whom I trust." For he will deliver you from the snare of the fowler and from*

---

[1] en.wikipedia.org/wiki/Need
[2] en.wikipedia.org/wiki/Maslow's_hierarchy_of_needs
[3] 2 Kings 6:26-27a
[4] Genesis 1:18

the deadly pestilence. He will cover you with his pinions, and under his wings you will find refuge; his faithfulness is a shield and buckler. You will not fear the terror of the night, nor the arrow that flies by day, nor the pestilence that stalks in darkness, nor the destruction that wastes at noonday.[5]

And my God will supply every need of yours according to his riches in glory in Christ Jesus.[6]

Jesus was clear that God understands what we need in the following passage from His sermon on the mount. Notice, He was not speaking of wants:

"Therefore I tell you, do not be anxious about your life, what you will eat or what you will drink, nor about your body, what you will put on. Is not life more than food, and the body more than clothing? Look at the birds of the air: they neither sow nor reap nor gather into barns, and yet your heavenly Father feeds them. Are you not of more value than they? And which of you by being anxious can add a single hour to his span of life? And why are you anxious about clothing? Consider the lilies of the field, how they grow: they neither toil nor spin, yet I tell you, even Solomon in all his glory was not arrayed like one of these. But if God so clothes the grass of the field, which today is alive and tomorrow is thrown into the oven, will he not much more clothe you, O you of little faith? Therefore do not be anxious, saying, 'What shall we eat?'

---

[5] Psalm 91:1-6
[6] Philippians 4:19

or 'What shall we drink?' or 'What shall we wear?' For
the Gentiles seek after all these things, and your heavenly
Father knows that you need them all. But seek first the
kingdom of God and his righteousness, and all these
things will be added to you. Therefore do not be anxious
about tomorrow, for tomorrow will be anxious for itself.
Sufficient for the day is its own trouble.[7]

Jesus' words from so long ago remain relevant today, as
reflected in these prophetic words from previous years:

November 2004: See and hear that I am God, for I
will be with you. In your time of need, My kingdom
is near. You will see My power; My plans will
unravel for you to see; you will see My power; you
will see My power. The time is coming; I am close.
Watch for me. I will beam down like the shinning
sun. I will bring healing with My wings, for I will
fulfill my word. I am coming with power. I will
pour out My spirit; I will save those who are lost,
for everyone will have a chance to see that I am
God.

September 2012: This is a funny angel: Rejoice,
rejoice, rejoice. We've given you the keys, we've
given you the words, we've given you the
strategies. Rejoice, rejoice and have fun. You need
laughter to shake off the seriousness. The world is
full of doom and gloom. Let us bring laughter, that

---

[7] Matthew 6:25-34

the world would know that God is on the throne and still in control. God is still on the throne; God is still Plan A. We need to bring joy, joy to the world. God has a plan. You know about the cloud, so follow the cloud and receive manna each day, each day, each day receive manna. Take enough just for today. Don't worry about tomorrow. Tomorrow will take care of tomorrow. Receive My joy, receive My joy, receive My joy. Look at what I'm doing. Don't look at what the enemy is doing.

December 2015: You will lack no good thing of all I have prepared. I would never hurt you; I would never leave you. Don't despair! For what you have lost now is little to compare with the plans I have for you My love.

Our greatest need, the one that surpasses all others, has already been taken care of for all who receive Jesus:

God shows his love for us in that while we were still sinners, Christ died for us. Since, therefore, we have now been justified by his blood, much more shall we be saved by him from the wrath of God. For if while we were enemies we were reconciled to God by the death of his Son, much more, now that we are reconciled, shall we be saved by his life. More than that, we also rejoice in God through our Lord Jesus Christ, through whom we have now received reconciliation.[8]

Yes, within the context of the amazing relationship that is available in Christ Jesus, our needs are supplied; but unless we grow in relationship with Him, we often do not understand the magnitude of His love and provision and sufficiency. So, there is a need on our part to pursue the things of God as passionately as we would pursue anything on earth; this is the true pursuit of happiness:

The way of the wicked is an abomination to the Lord, but he loves him who pursues righteousness.[9]

Whoever pursues righteousness and kindness will find life, righteousness, and honor.[10]

Listen to me, you who pursue righteousness, you who seek the Lord: look to the rock from which you were hewn, and to the quarry from which you were dug.[11]

So then let us pursue what makes for peace and for mutual upbuilding.[12]

Pursue love, and earnestly desire the spiritual gifts, especially that you may prophesy.[13]

---

[8] Roman 5:8-11
[9] Proverbs 15:9
[10] Proverbs 21:21
[11] Isaiah 51:1
[12] Romans 14:19
[13] 1 Corinthians 14:1

> *But as for you, O man of God, flee these things. Pursue righteousness, godliness, faith, love, steadfastness, gentleness.*[14]

> *So flee youthful passions and pursue righteousness, faith, love, and peace, along with those who call on the Lord from a pure heart.*[15]

> *For "Whoever desires to love life and see good days, let him keep his tongue from evil and his lips from speaking deceit; let him turn away from evil and do good; let him seek peace and pursue it. For the eyes of the Lord are on the righteous, and his ears are open to their prayer. But the face of the Lord is against those who do evil."* [16]

There remain many things we need to understand about our God, with even the most knowledgeable Christians among us still only having scraped the surface of His mysteries. He is, and will always remain, beyond our complete understanding:

> *For my thoughts are not your thoughts, neither are your ways my ways, declares the Lord. For as the heavens are higher than the earth, so are my ways higher than your ways and my thoughts than your thoughts.*[17]

---

[14] 1 Timothy 6:11
[15] 2 Timothy 2:22
[16] 1 Peter 3:10-12
[17] Isaiah 55:8-9

For one who speaks in a tongue speaks not to men but to God; for no one understands him, but he utters mysteries in the Spirit.[18]

How easy it is to hand out well-meant advice regarding what others need to do in their Christian walk. Perhaps we forget that God speaks to each one individually, and our response to Him doesn't necessarily need to align with what others think we should do. Rather, it should be about what He directs us to do. Paul relates the following experience:

I have a prophet friend who stayed at my house and observed me; this person said that I needed to have more soaking music playing. I love worship in the services but obedience is worship, so I try to do what the Lord wants me to do. I need to do what the Lord tells me to do.

Fortunately, the Holy Spirit is always there to direct and teach us all that we need to know, when we need to know it:

O Lord, you have searched me and known me! You know when I sit down and when I rise up; you discern my thoughts from afar. You search out my path and my lying down and are acquainted with all my ways. Even before a word is on my tongue, behold, O Lord, you know it altogether. You hem me in, behind and before, and lay

---

[18] 1 Corinthians 14:2

your hand upon me. Such knowledge is too wonderful for me; it is high; I cannot attain it.

Where shall I go from your Spirit? Or where shall I flee from your presence? If I ascend to heaven, you are there! If I make my bed in Sheol, you are there! If I take the wings of the morning and dwell in the uttermost parts of the sea, even there your hand shall lead me, and your right hand shall hold me. If I say, "Surely the darkness shall cover me, and the light about me be night," even the darkness is not dark to you; the night is bright as the day, for darkness is as light with you.[19]

But the anointing that you received from him abides in you, and you have no need that anyone should teach you. But as his anointing teaches you about everything, and is true, and is no lie—just as it has taught you, abide in him. [20]

Sometimes we get so hungry for a new move of the Spirit that we fall into the trap of thinking we need to go back and re-capture a past move of God, rather than integrating those valuable lessons into the new thing God is doing:

Behold, I am doing a new thing; now it springs forth, do you not perceive it?

Peter did it on the mountain of transfiguration when he wanted to build three tents for Jesus, Moses and Elijah. We do it when we try to re-capture such extraordinary revivals

---

[19] Psalm 139:1-12
[20]1 John 2:27

as Azusa Street, the Jesus Movement, or the Toronto Blessing. We'd do well to remember that His presence and instruction is available each day:

> *The Lord God has given me the tongue of those who are taught, that I may know how to sustain with a word him who is weary. Morning by morning he awakens; he awakens my ear to hear as those who are taught. The Lord God has opened my ear, and I was not rebellious; I turned not backward.*[21]

> *But this I call to mind, and therefore I have hope: The steadfast love of the Lord never ceases; his mercies never come to an end; they are new every morning; great is your faithfulness. "The Lord is my portion," says my soul, "therefore I will hope in him."* [22]

A word from 2012, sums up well the difference between what we think we need, versus what we need to do:

> There's wisdom knocking at the door; for those who hear it will be well. It will be well. So, listen well for wisdom and it will be well, led by revelation and not the need of man. The poor you will have with you always; the needy and the orphan you will have always, but we are only to do what the Father is asking us to do. We are to be led only by the Spirit and not by need. The King of Kings did not feel guilty or ashamed because He passed by a beggar,

---

[21] Isaiah 50:4-5
[22] Lamentations 3:21-24

because it was not the time. I'm building a net but it's a new net; it's a new net. Rest in Me, rest in Me, for revelation to build; for I am the Master Builder and I know what I'm doing.

CHAPTER SEVEN:
LACK

The implication of lack is that something is still needed; there is a deficiency of some kind. It follows that since some needs are justified, so are some things (both physical and spiritual) subject to lack, as scriptures illustrate:

> *Afterward, when David heard of it, he said, "I and my kingdom are forever guiltless before the Lord for the blood of Abner the son of Ner. May it fall upon the head of Joab and upon all his father's house, and may the house of Joab never be without one who has a discharge or who is leprous or who holds a spindle or who falls by the sword or who lacks bread!"* [1]

> *And a ruler asked him, "Good Teacher, what must I do to inherit eternal life?" And Jesus said to him, "Why do you call me good? No one is good except God alone. You know the commandments: 'Do not commit adultery, Do not murder, Do not steal, Do not bear false witness, Honor your father and mother.'" And he said, "All these I have kept from my youth." When Jesus heard this, he said to him, "One thing you still lack. Sell all that you have and distribute to the poor, and you will have treasure in heaven; and come, follow me."* [2]

---

[1] 2 Samuel 3:28-29
[2] Luke 18:18-22

So receive him in the Lord with all joy, and honor such men, for he nearly died for the work of Christ, risking his life to complete what was lacking in your service to me.[3]

For this very reason, make every effort to supplement your faith with virtue, and virtue with knowledge, and knowledge with self-control, and self-control with steadfastness, and steadfastness with godliness, and godliness with brotherly affection, and brotherly affection with love. For if these qualities are yours and are increasing, they keep you from being ineffective or unfruitful in the knowledge of our Lord Jesus Christ.[4]

The Bible makes it clear that true lack is often the result of sinful behavior:

He who commits adultery lacks sense; he who does it destroys himself.[5]

"I gave you cleanness of teeth in all your cities, and lack of bread in all your places, yet you did not return to me," declares the Lord.[6]

A prophetic word illustrates how the enemy has worked to instill lack:

The accuser speaks to claim what is yours; he created a false need of lack to have what you

---

[3] Philippians 2:29-30
[4] 1 Peter 1:5-9
[5] Proverbs 6:32
[6] Amos 4:6

thought was needed instead of what was originally that. You have all that is needed pertaining to life and godliness, but lack holds you back to try to gain what you lost.

Such deception! We believe the lies of the enemy, so our perceived lack holds us back from the blessings that God stands ready to deliver. Remember the prodigal son? He fell into the trap of believing that he knew what was needed, and learned the hard way that his perception was false. His story illustrates the loving kindness of the Father to receive us, and to reverse the dire consequences of lack that have occurred because of our sin:

> And he said, "There was a man who had two sons. And the younger of them said to his father, 'Father, give me the share of property that is coming to me.' And he divided his property between them. Not many days later, the younger son gathered all he had and took a journey into a far country, and there he squandered his property in reckless living. And when he had spent everything, a severe famine arose in that country, and he began to be in need. So he went and hired himself out to one of the citizens of that country, who sent him into his fields to feed pigs. And he was longing to be fed with the pods that the pigs ate, and no one gave him anything.

> "But when he came to himself, he said, 'How many of my father's hired servants have more than enough bread, but I perish here with hunger! I will arise and go to my father, and I will say to him, "Father, I have sinned against

heaven and before you. I am no longer worthy to be called your son. Treat me as one of your hired servants."' And he arose and came to his father. But while he was still a long way off, his father saw him and felt compassion, and ran and embraced him and kissed him. And the son said to him, 'Father, I have sinned against heaven and before you. I am no longer worthy to be called your son.' But the father said to his servants, 'Bring quickly the best robe, and put it on him, and put a ring on his hand, and shoes on his feet. And bring the fattened calf and kill it, and let us eat and celebrate. For this my son was dead, and is alive again; he was lost, and is found.' And they began to celebrate." [7]

In the same way that the prodigal son remembered the good things that his father supplied, we should also recall God's promises and provision. The Israelites were also reminded of this truth:

For the Lord your God has blessed you in all the work of your hands. He knows your going through this great wilderness. These forty years the Lord your God has been with you. You have lacked nothing."' [8]

During the time of the early church it is clear that unity, love, unselfishness, and a righteous lifestyle according to what had been taught by the apostles was key to an absence of lack:

---

[7] Luke 15:11-24
[8] Deuteronomy 2:7

Now the full number of those who believed were of one heart and soul, and no one said that any of the things that belonged to him was his own, but they had everything in common. And with great power the apostles were giving their testimony to the resurrection of the Lord Jesus, and great grace was upon them all. There was not a needy person among them, for as many as were owners of lands or houses sold them and brought the proceeds of what was sold and laid it at the apostles' feet, and it was distributed to each as any had need.[9]

Now concerning brotherly love you have no need for anyone to write to you, for you yourselves have been taught by God to love one another, for that indeed is what you are doing to all the brothers throughout Macedonia. But we urge you, brothers, to do this more and more, and to aspire to live quietly, and to mind your own affairs, and to work with your hands, as we instructed you, so that you may walk properly before outsiders and be dependent on no one.[10]

We are so fortunate that God loves us so much that all we need to do is trust Him and ask; He is there, waiting to provide:

---

[9] Acts 4:32-35
[10] 1 Thessalonians 4:9-12

If any of you lacks wisdom, let him ask God, who gives generously to all without reproach, and it will be given him.[11]

Rejoice in the Lord always; again I will say, rejoice. Let your reasonableness be known to everyone. The Lord is at hand; do not be anxious about anything, but in everything by prayer and supplication with thanksgiving let your requests be made known to God. And the peace of God, which surpasses all understanding, will guard your hearts and your minds in Christ Jesus..[12]

Unfortunately, whether Old Testament, New Testament or current day, mankind has been/is notorious for falling prey to the enemy's deceptive tactics, ending up in the previously quoted spiral of destruction:

It's a very, very sad thing to watch; it is hard to watch a loved one or friend implode because they have come to expect their wants and needs to be met so they will have no lack. One thing leads to another, spiraling down a rabbit hole.

Want becomes need; need becomes lack; and false expectations are the end result.

---

[11] James 1:5
[12] Philippians 4:4-7

CHAPTER EIGHT:
EXPECT

We lived in a small, lumber-company-owned town, equipped with a three-room schoolhouse for first through sixth grades; three teachers taught two grades per classroom. Nobody in our town had ever attended kindergarten, and I was to be the first; the only catch was I'd have to ride a bus into town, which was about 30 minutes away, a big deal in those days. My best friend was beginning first grade and I'd have no one to play with, so I was very excited to be able to start school too. It all began so wonderfully; my mother took me that first day, my teacher was young and pretty and kind, and the activities with the other kids were lots of fun. This was going to be great! Then instead of riding home with Mom, I was allowed to ride the school bus — more excitement!

BUT... Five years old, and I was about to learn on the second day of kindergarten that life doesn't always live up to our expectations. About halfway home, the bus driver said this was the last stop and everyone had to get off; I did with much fear and confusion. Fortunately, I discovered that my mother was driving right behind us, so she put me in the car and talked to the driver. Apparently, nobody had told him the route would be extended into our town; they got it sorted out by the following day, and Mom walked me to the bus stop. I was excited again, BUT only for the duration of the ride. When we arrived at school I went directly to my room, BUT was immediately escorted to a different class; they said the first room assignment had been a mistake. I was devastated; suddenly nothing was familiar, the teacher seemed really old and grumpy, and it was a whole new batch of kids who didn't seem to like me; I sat lonely and sad at a table all by myself, trying not to cry. My expectations for kindergarten did me in, and in retrospect the trauma of those two days affected my entire school experience and required inner healing many years later.

We're all guilty of expecting something to be more than it turns out to be. Those things for which we dream from childhood through our senior-citizenry often fall short of expectations, and disappointments pile up. Pip, the main character of Charles Dickens' novel, *Great Expectations*, provides a fictional but true-to-life example. He thought the fortune he'd inherited from a secret benefactor would open the door to marrying the girl of his dreams. BUT...Ultimately, Pip discovered was not necessarily the key ingredient for his happiness and realized that his expectations had robbed him of an appreciation of the relationship s and other blessings in his life.

Our expectations reflect those things we consider likely to occur, and when they don't turn out the way we thought, the result may range from mild disappointment to severe depression, disillusionment, and loss of hope and faith. There can be a vast divide between the expectations of what is likely to happen versus the reality of what does happen, and if our hope lies anywhere other than in the unchanging nature and promises of God, we will struggle to cope with life. His promises are the only thing in life on which we can build our expectations because:

Jesus Christ is the same yesterday and today and forever.[1]

Every good gift and every perfect gift is from above, coming down from the Father of lights, with whom there is no variation or shadow due to change.[2]

God is not man, that he should lie, or a son of man, that he should change his mind. Has he said, and will he not do it? Or has he spoken, and will he not fulfill it?[3]

The counsel of the LORD stands forever, the plans of his heart to all generations.[4]

The Bible illustrates dramatic differences in what the righteous and wicked can expect from God, which should make one wonder why anyone would choose evil instead of righteousness:

The hope of the righteous brings joy, but the expectation of the wicked will perish.[5]

When the wicked dies, his hope will perish, and the expectation of wealth perishes too. The righteous is

---

[1] Hebrews 13:8
[2] James 1:17
[3] Numbers 23:19
[4] Psalm 33:11
[5] Proverbs 10:28

delivered from trouble, and the wicked walks into it instead. [6]

The desire of the righteous ends only in good, the expectation of the wicked in wrath. [7]

They have seen false visions and lying divinations. They say, 'Declares the LORD,' when the LORD has not sent them, and yet they expect him to fulfill their word. Have you not seen a false vision and uttered a lying divination, whenever you have said, 'Declares the LORD,' although I have not spoken?" Therefore thus says the Lord GOD: "Because you have uttered falsehood and seen lying visions, therefore behold, I am against you, declares the Lord GOD. My hand will be against the prophets who see false visions and who give lying divinations. They shall not be in the council of my people, nor be enrolled in the register of the house of Israel, nor shall they enter the land of Israel. And you shall know that I am the Lord GOD. [8]

Therefore, stay awake, for you do not know on what day your Lord is coming...Therefore you also must be ready, for the Son of Man is coming at an hour you do not expect...Blessed is that servant whom his master will find so doing when he comes. Truly, I say to you, he will set him over all his possessions. But if that wicked servant says to himself, 'My master is delayed,' and begins to beat his fellow servants and eats and drinks

---

[6] Proverbs 11:7–8
[7] Proverbs 11:23
[8] Ezekiel 13:6–9

with drunkards, the master of that servant will come on a day when he does not expect him and at an hour he does not know and will cut him in pieces and put him with the hypocrites. In that place there will be weeping and gnashing of teeth.[9]

For if we go on sinning deliberately after receiving the knowledge of the truth, there no longer remains a sacrifice for sins, but a fearful expectation of judgment, and a fury of fire that will consume the adversaries.[10]

From Genesis to Revelation, there is no question that the Lord rewards those who are faithful to Him, whether they expect it or not:

Now the eyes of Israel were dim with age, so that he could not see. So Joseph brought them near him, and he kissed them and embraced them. And Israel said to Joseph, "I never expected to see your face; and behold, God has let me see your offspring also."[11]

When Peter came to himself, he said, "Now I am sure that the Lord has sent his angel and rescued me from the hand of Herod and from all that the Jewish people were expecting." [12]

For they gave according to their means, as I can testify, and beyond their means, of their own accord, begging us

---

[9] Matthew 24:42, 44, 46–51
[10] Hebrews 10:26–27
[11] Genesis 48:10–11
[12] Acts 12:11

earnestly for the favor of taking part in the relief of the saints — and this, not as we expected, but they gave themselves first to the Lord and then by the will of God to us.[13]

Then the angel showed me the river of the water of life, bright as crystal, flowing from the throne of God and of the Lamb through the middle of the street of the city; also, on either side of the river, the tree of life with its twelve kinds of fruit, yielding its fruit each month. The leaves of the tree were for the healing of the nations. No longer will there be anything accursed, but the throne of God and of the Lamb will be in it, and his servants will worship him. They will see his face, and his name will be on their foreheads. And night will be no more. They will need no light of lamp or sun, for the Lord God will be their light, and they will reign forever and ever. [14]

The promises that abound throughout God's word are the expectations for which we can hope; and when we do we can proclaim with the Apostle Paul:

Yes, and I will rejoice, for I know that through your prayers and the help of the Spirit of Jesus Christ this will turn out for my deliverance, as it is my eager expectation and hope that I will not be at all ashamed, but that with full courage now as always Christ will be honored in my

---

[13] 2 Corinthians 8:3–5
[14] Revelation 22:1–5

body, whether by life or by death. For to me to live is Christ, and to die is gain.[15]

---

[15] Philippians 1:18-21

CHAPTER NINE:
THE ANCIENT PATHS

"Houston, we've got a problem," is a saying, lifted from the dialogue between Command Module Pilot Jack Swigert and the NASA support staff on earth, as he advised them that Apollo 13 was in serious trouble.[1] Today, it is often used to introduce an unforeseen problem. Sadly, any problem those astronauts encountered pales in comparison to the one every person on earth has shared since the beginning of time; since Adam and Eve were deceived and led down a garden path, to use another idiom. Then they were required to leave the actual Garden of Eden for they had wandered off of the ancient path of the Lord.[2]

As discussed earlier, the primary issue we have faced since the very first sin is fear; but it was never God's plan. Rather, He has always desired for us to experience the polar opposite of fear, which is His peace and rest. It may sound simplistic, but the choice is ours`:

> *Thus says the LORD: "Stand by the roads, and look, and ask for the ancient paths, where the good way is; and walk in it, and find rest for your souls. But they said, 'We will not walk in it.'*[3]

---

[1] history.nasa.gov/ep76.pdf
[2] Ancient pathways were discussed in chapter five of *Exploring Heavenly Places: A Travelogue of Heavenly Journeys: Volume 10*
[3] Jeremiah 6:16

The Hebrew word for 'ancient' is *olam*, which means:

> 1 long duration, antiquity, futurity, for ever, ever, everlasting, evermore, perpetual, old, ancient, world. 1A ancient time, long time (of past). 1B (of future). *1B1* for ever, always. *1B2* continuous existence, perpetual. *1B3* everlasting, indefinite or unending future, eternity. [4]

It is a path that connects us to eternity; it is the way of wisdom; it is the good way, which the Bible often describes:

> *You make known to me the path of life; in your presence there is fullness of joy; at your right hand are pleasures forevermore.* [5]

> *All the paths of the LORD are steadfast love and faithfulness, for those who keep his covenant and his testimonies.*[6]

> *Blessed is the one who finds wisdom, and the one who gets understanding, for the gain from her is better than gain from silver and her profit better than gold. She is more precious than jewels, and nothing you desire can compare with her. Long life is in her right hand; in her left hand are riches and honor. Her ways are ways of pleasantness, and all her paths are peace.* [7]

---

[4] Strong, J. (1995). *Enhanced Strong's Lexicon*. Woodside Bible Fellowship.
[5] Psalm 16:11.
[6] Psalm 25:10
[7] Proverbs 3:13–17

This is God's original intention; it is His desire for us. But the way of the world is to walk away from the ancient paths because the enemy has lured mankind deeply into the lie that we can be self-sufficient. We've come to believe that we can determine our own paths through self-realization and determination, or through good thoughts and words and works. We have come to trust in education, jobs, wealth and power in our quest for success. But it's an empty journey without God leading the way, and many end up trying to obtain peace in everything from healthy eating and exercise to drugs and alcohol. Or vacations — surely a beautiful, quiet beach or a snowy ski resort will help; but no, for fear doesn't stay behind at home. None of it works, because it is all based on the original lie that man doesn't need God.

The enemy's way is one that leads us along his paths of unrighteousness, his ancient paths of evil where there is no peace:

> *Will you keep to the old way that wicked men have trod? They were snatched away before their time; their foundation was washed away.* [8]

> *Transgression speaks to the wicked deep in his heart; there is no fear of God before his eyes. For he flatters himself in his own eyes that his iniquity cannot be found out and hated. The words of his mouth are trouble and deceit; he has ceased to act wisely and do good. He plots*

---

[8] Job 22:15–16

trouble while on his bed; he sets himself in a way that is not good; he does not reject evil. [9]

Their feet run to evil, and they are swift to shed innocent blood; their thoughts are thoughts of iniquity; desolation and destruction are in their highways. The way of peace they do not know, and there is no justice in their paths; they have made their roads crooked; no one who treads on them knows peace. [10]

But my people have forgotten me; they make offerings to false gods; they made them stumble in their ways, in the ancient roads, and to walk into side roads, not the highway, making their land a horror, a thing to be hissed at forever. Everyone who passes by it is horrified and shakes his head. [11]

None is righteous, no, not one; no one understands; no one seeks for God. All have turned aside; together they have become worthless; no one does good, not even one."

Their throat is an open grave; they use their tongues to deceive. The venom of asps is under their lips. Their mouth is full of curses and bitterness. Their feet are swift to shed blood; in their paths are ruin and misery, and the way of peace they have not known." There is no fear of God before their eyes."[12]

---

[9] Psalm 36:1–4
[10] Isaiah 59:7–8
[11] Jeremiah 18:15–16
[12] Romans 3:10–18

Nowadays, there is a popular teaching within the Church that since God's grace is sufficient and covers all of our transgressions, we've got nothing to worry about. True, at least in terms of eternal life, but to live a victorious life that's full of peace and rest in the here-and-now, ongoing obedience is required. The Lord expects us to live according to His standards of righteousness — His commandments — even though we are no longer bound by the Law. In fact, when we refuse to follow His commandments, fear is the constant threat:

> *Your life shall hang in doubt before you. Night and day you shall be in dread and have no assurance of your life. In the morning you shall say, 'If only it were evening!' and at evening you shall say, 'If only it were morning!' because of the dread that your heart shall feel, and the sights that your eyes shall see.*[13]

In Eden, disobedience caused the way to the tree of life to be blocked, but obedience to God's command to believe on the Lord Jesus Christ paves the way to the tree of life when we accept Him as our Savior:

> *Blessed are those who wash their robes, so that they may have the right to the tree of life and that they may enter the city by the gates.* [14]

But we can't stop there. The ancient paths are the way of the Lord; they are the paths on which we walk when we trust

---

[13] Deuteronomy 28:66–67
[14] Revelation 22:14

God to lead, no matter what; they are where we say no to the situational ethics of the world and choose to live God's way. Just because Adam and Eve, the Children of Israel and many others down through the generations have made the tragic decision to reject God's ways doesn't mean we have to, and the Bible teaches us how not to stray:

> *Trust in the LORD with all your heart, and do not lean on your own understanding. In all your ways acknowledge him, and he will make straight your paths.*[15]

> *I have taught you the way of wisdom; I have led you in the paths of uprightness. When you walk, your step will not be hampered, and if you run, you will not stumble. Keep hold of instruction; do not let go; guard her, for she is your life. Do not enter the path of the wicked, and do not walk in the way of the evil. Avoid it; do not go on it; turn away from it and pass on.*[16]

> *Trust in the LORD, and do good; dwell in the land and befriend faithfulness. Delight yourself in the LORD, and he will give you the desires of your heart. Commit your way to the LORD; trust in him, and he will act. He will bring forth your righteousness as the light, and your justice as the noonday. Be still before the LORD and wait patiently for him; fret not yourself over the one who*

---

[15] Proverbs 3:5–6
[16] Proverbs 4:11–15

prospers in his way, over the man who carries out evil devices!. [17]

Wonderful promises are attached to our choice to travel on the righteous pathways of the Lord:

Blessed is the man who walks not in the counsel of the wicked, nor stands in the way of sinners, nor sits in the seat of scoffers; but his delight is in the law of the LORD, and on his law he meditates day and night. He is like a tree planted by streams of water that yields its fruit in its season, and its leaf does not wither. In all that he does, he prospers. The wicked are not so, but are like chaff that the wind drives away. Therefore the wicked will not stand in the judgment, nor sinners in the congregation of the righteous; for the LORD knows the way of the righteous, but the way of the wicked will perish. [18]

I have taught you the way of wisdom; I have led you in the paths of uprightness. When you walk, your step will not be hampered, and if you run, you will not stumble. [19]

On April 5, 2020, I wrote in my journal:

This morning my attention was caught as never before by the words in 1 John 2:1 describing our advocate with the Father as, "Jesus Christ the righteous". It's reminiscent of the way some earthly kings have been referenced historically; kings such

---

[17] Psalm 37:3–7
[18] Psalm 1:1–6
[19] Proverbs 4:11–12

as Richard the Lionhearted, Alexander the Great, Vlad the Impaler, Edward the Elder, or William the Conqueror. But none can compare to Jesus the Righteous! I am also focused not only on His righteousness but also on how we are to practice righteousness:

> *Little children, let no one deceive you. Whoever practices righteousness is righteous, as he is righteous. Whoever makes a practice of sinning is of the devil, for the devil has been sinning from the beginning. The reason the Son of God appeared was to destroy the works of the devil.*[20]

I think of professionals who practice medicine or law, and ponder how Christians should practice righteousness just as diligently. There's an old saying that practice makes perfect, and nowhere could it apply more accurately than it does when we persistently practice His righteousness, enter into and share His perfection.

Jesus the Righteous, the Prince of Peace, is always with us. As we walk with Him along His pathways, all of the fear that fuels ungodly want, need, lack and false expectations drowns in a sea of rest and peace.

---

[20] 1 John 3:7–8

Chapter Ten:
But, But, But...

Television, Internet, newspapers, any media; on any given day, take your pick and the news will be full of frightening things—violence, deception and dissention, hurricanes, fires, scandals, unemployment, and the list goes on. Jesus' return seems to be rapidly approaching, though only God knows exactly where we are in terms of end times. That said, we're certainly far enough along for people to be overcome with negative emotions, and fear tops the list, accompanied by hopelessness, anxiety, depression, worry, to name a few. But, when Jesus explained what end times would look like to His disciples, He said that these things should not be frightening:

> *And Jesus answered them, "See that no one leads you astray. For many will come in my name, saying, 'I am the Christ,' and they will lead many astray. And you will hear of wars and rumors of wars. <u>See that you are not alarmed</u>, for this must take place, but the end is not yet. For nation will rise against nation, and kingdom against kingdom, and there will be famines and earthquakes in various places. All these are but the beginning of the birth pains. "Then they will deliver you up to tribulation and put you to death, and you will be hated by all nations for my name's sake. And then many will fall away and betray one another and hate one another. And many false prophets will arise and lead many astray. And because*

lawlessness will be increased, the love of many will grow cold.[1]

He must have been kidding!!! How could knowledge of such a dire future be comforting? Because it comes with His promise:

But the one who endures to the end will be saved. And this gospel of the kingdom will be proclaimed throughout the whole world as a testimony to all nations, and then the end will come. [2]

Somewhere along the way, deception and manipulation seem to have become acceptable behavior in order to achieve a goal, so how can we trust anyone anymore? Some might even ask how we can trust what Jesus said? How do we know that He was any different than our people today who twist the facts to serve their own purposes? How do we know that He was telling the truth? What's His track record? Are we really supposed to believe that we don't need to worry? That doesn't seem logical, or even possible. And, how in the world can we be expected to choose God's pathways? Isn't life just too hard for that?

Evidence that God's word is true is overwhelming, and many volumes have been written documenting fulfilled prophecies and promises. So let's narrow it down and get specific regarding His track record with people that He told

---

[1] Matthew 24:4-12
[2] Matthew 24:13-14

not to fear. Is there proof that He came through for them and that He kept His word? Yes!

Abram was already 75 years old when God told him to pack up, leave his home, and go to another country; all based on His promise that, "I will make of you a great nation." Years passed; difficult years of battles fought, famine, fear, family friction; and years in which the God-promised heir of whom a great nation would come was not conceived:

> *After these things the word of the Lord came to Abram in a vision, saying, "Do not be afraid, Abram. I am your shield, your exceedingly great reward."*[3]

More difficult and disappointing years passed before Isaac finally came along; by which time Abram, renamed Abraham, was 100 years old. Yet, through all of the trials, he steadfastly chose to believe God and to continue on in faith.

Isaac had grown up and married when there was another famine, and God showed up to restate the promise he'd made to Abraham and remind him not to fear:

> *And the Lord appeared to him and said, "… I will be with you and will bless you, for to you and to your offspring I will give all these lands, and I will establish the oath that I swore to Abraham your father. I will multiply your offspring as the stars of heaven and will give to your*

---

[3] Genesis 15:1

offspring all these lands. And in your offspring all the nations of the earth shall be blessed, because Abraham obeyed my voice and kept my charge, my commandments, my statutes, and my laws." ... And the Lord appeared to him the same night and said, "I am the God of Abraham your father. Fear not, for I am with you and will bless you and multiply your offspring for my servant Abraham's sake."[4]

Eventually, Isaac's son, Jacob, had his own encounter with God:

Then God spoke to Israel in the visions of the night, and said, "Jacob, Jacob!" And he said, "Here I am." So He said, "I am God, the God of your father; do not fear to go down to Egypt, for I will make of you a great nation there. I will go down with you to Egypt, and I will also surely bring you up again; and Joseph will put his hand on your eyes."[5]

Fast forward to Joshua, just after Moses' death. Here he was, 80 years old and taking over the leadership of the Children of Israel, with years of battle ahead in order to seize the land of Canaan. Talk about someone who could've been frightened—there were giants in that land, and 40 years earlier all of the Israelites except Joshua and Caleb had been so scared that they'd refused to go forward, and ended up wandering around the desert until they all died and a

---

[4] Genesis 26:2a, 3b-5, 24
[5] Genesis 46:2-4

younger-and-braver generation grew up. Surely a bit of fear could be expected?

> *Have I not commanded you? Be strong and of good courage; <u>do not be afraid</u>, nor be dismayed, for the Lord your God is with you wherever you go."*[6]

After Joshua's death, the Lord raised up judges, who saved them out of the hand of those who plundered them. Along came Gideon, and one day an angel showed up with the news that God was calling him to undertake the thankless task of leading this unrighteous bunch:

> *Then Gideon perceived that he was the angel of the Lord. And Gideon said, "Alas, O Lord God! For now I have seen the angel of the Lord face to face." But the Lord said to him, "Peace be to you. <u>Do not fear</u>; you shall not die."*[7]

How about some prophets? Jeremiah and Ezekiel were both commissioned by God to warn His hard-hearted people that they were headed for destruction — not a fun job, to say the least. They would be commanded by God to perform seemingly outrageous prophetic acts; they would be ignored, ridiculed and there would be a constant risk of persecution. How difficult it would be to remain on God's righteous pathways without fear:

> *But the Lord said to me, "Do not say, 'I am only a youth'; or to all to whom I send you, you shall go, and whatever*

---

[6] Joshua 1:8-10
[7] Judges 6:22-23

I command you, you shall speak. <u>Do not be afraid</u> of them, for I am with you to deliver you, declares the Lord."[8]

And you, son of man, <u>be not afraid of them,</u> nor be afraid of their words, though briers and thorns are with you and you sit on scorpions. <u>Be not afraid</u> of their words, <u>nor be dismayed</u> at their looks, for they are a rebellious house.[9]

Abraham, Isaac and Jacob; Joshua; Gideon; Jeremiah and Ezekiel; all were told by God to not be afraid in the face of tremendous trials. Oh, but they were Bible heroes — they were special — right? No, they were ordinary men; the only thing that made them any different than others is that they made a choice to believe that God would be faithful to His promises. They all chose faith over fear. They all understood the truth of words that had not yet even been written by Paul the Apostle

Therefore, since we have been justified by faith, we have peace with God through our Lord Jesus Christ. Through him we have also obtained access by faith into this grace in which we stand, and we rejoice in hope of the glory of God. Not only that, we rejoice in our sufferings, knowing that suffering produces endurance, and endurance produces character, and character produces hope, and hope does not put us to shame, because God's love has

---

[8] Jeremiah 1:7-9
[9] Ezekiel 2:6

been poured into our hearts through the Holy Spirit who has been given to us.[10]

Still, they lived so long ago in Old Testament times; surely things are different now. No, not unless we choose to ignore Jesus, who repeatedly encouraged His followers, "Why are you so afraid?" "Take courage." "Don't be afraid." "Why did you doubt, you of little faith?" "Do you still have no faith? It is I—don't be afraid."

So here we are, living in difficult, disheartening and even frightening times; and like those Old Testament believers, we have a choice. We can dwell in the mire of fear, or we can exercise our faith in God, for He can be trusted to keep His promises.

But the Lord is faithful. He will establish you and guard you against the evil one.[11]

---

[10] Romans 5: 1-5
[11] 2 Thessalonians 3:3

Chapter Eleven:
God Understands

In the midst of our pain, God is here—always! And He has shown me anew just how close He is today.

Reading my Bible, and journaling with a heavy heart, I pondered why I felt so down. A lot is going on, but I couldn't put my finger on it. Certainly, chaos and fear has invaded our nation and we are embroiled in the run-up to the 2020 presidential election, which is both concerning and irritating, but that wasn't it. I have a long list of things that don't seem to be getting done as quickly as I'd like, but that wasn't it.

My son called last night, sobbing, because their precious beagle, Sidney, is terminally ill and my ten-year-old grandson is having an especially hard time dealing with it. Not only is my baby hurting but so are his babies, and any mother and/or grandmother knows how a call like that will tear at your heart. It hurt, but wasn't the whole reason for my discomfort.

I considered my life, and related to the psalmists in terms of the brevity of life as well as any impact that I might make for God on succeeding generations:

O God, from my youth you have taught me, and I still proclaim your wondrous deeds. So even to old age and gray hairs, O God, do not forsake me, until I proclaim your might to another generation, your power to all those to come. [1]

O LORD, make me know my end and what is the measure of my days; let me know how fleeting I am! Behold, you have made my days a few handbreadths, and my lifetime is as nothing before you. Surely all mankind stands as a mere breath! Selah

Surely a man goes about as a shadow! Surely for nothing they are in turmoil; man heaps up wealth and does not know who will gather! "And now, O Lord, for what do I wait? My hope is in you. [2]

My need today was something I really couldn't nail down right away, but then I received a text from my son that they are taking Sidney to the vet today to put her down, and I was suddenly encompassed by grief; tears filled my eyes, and a terrible sorrow came upon me. I didn't understand the intensity of my reaction, which was quite unusual for me. As much as I loved my parents, I didn't even feel this way when they died; it was different somehow.

After an hour or so, the intense grief suddenly lifted, and I understood. What I'd been feeling was God's heart for His people when they are hurting; it was His way of reminding me that yes, He does understand, He does care, and He is merciful. I knew without a doubt that the depth of His sorrow that I felt today is not something I could endure for

---

[1] Psalm 71:17–18
[2] Psalm 39:4–7

very long without drowning in a pool of depression and hopelessness. Praise the Lord that He understands and feels our deepest needs because He's been there, done that:

> For we do not have a high priest who is unable to sympathize with our weaknesses, but one who in every respect has been tempted as we are, yet without sin. [16] Let us then with confidence draw near to the throne of grace, that we may receive mercy and find grace to help in time of need. [3]

> In the days of his flesh, Jesus offered up prayers and supplications, with loud cries and tears, to him who was able to save him from death, and he was heard because of his reverence. Although he was a son, he learned obedience through what he suffered. And being made perfect, he became the source of eternal salvation to all who obey him, being designated by God a high priest after the order of Melchizedek. [4]

Jesus endured suffering that far exceeds anything that will ever be required of us, yet He never once abandoned God's ancient pathways. Instead of succumbing to the temptation of the enemy's version of fear, He regularly practiced the fear of the Lord. In the scripture above, the Greek word for

---

[3] Hebrews 4:15–16
[4] Hebrews 5:7–10

'reverence' is *eulabeia,* meaning reverent awe in the presence of God, awe, the fear of God.[5]

> *Blessed is everyone who fears the LORD, who walks in his ways! You shall eat the fruit of the labor of your hands; you shall be blessed, and it shall be well with you. Your wife will be like a fruitful vine within your house; your children will be like olive shoots around your table. Behold, thus shall the man be blessed who fears the LORD. The LORD bless you from Zion! May you see the prosperity of Jerusalem all the days of your life! May you see your children's children! Peace be upon Israel!* [6]

> *the fear of the LORD is clean, enduring forever; the rules of the LORD are true, and righteous altogether.* [7]

> *The fear of the LORD is the beginning of wisdom; all those who practice it have a good understanding. His praise endures forever!* [8]

> *The fear of the LORD is the beginning of knowledge; fools despise wisdom and instruction.* [9]

---

[5] Arndt, W., Danker, F. W., Bauer, W., & Gingrich, F. W. (2000). *A Greek-English lexicon of the New Testament and other early Christian literature* (3rd ed., p. 407). Chicago: University of Chicago Press.
[6] Psalms 128:1–6
[7] Psalms 19:9
[8] Psalms 111:10
[9] Proverbs 1:7

The end of the matter; all has been heard. Fear God and keep his commandments, for this is the whole duty of man.[10]

The fear of the Lord is one of seven Spirits of the Lord, in whom Jesus delighted:

There shall come forth a shoot from the stump of Jesse, and a branch from his roots shall bear fruit. And the Spirit of the LORD shall rest upon him, the Spirit of wisdom and understanding, the Spirit of counsel and might, the Spirit of knowledge and the fear of the LORD. And his delight shall be in the fear of the LORD. [11]

In 2008, we received a prophetic word that is quite applicable to this discussion:

Fear of the Lord leads to knowledge; it is in the knowing. I will show you a mystery; it is the path of righteousness. It is a higher way to higher ways. There is more of Me than you have ever believed. This is holy, a holy path. There are wonders to behold. If you will choose this path, you will be tested; but I am faithful. If you say yes, I will direct your steps.

Yes, we will be tested, but so was Jesus; yet He trusted His Father in the midst of His worst moments. We must keep in mind the fact that He refused fear does not mean He

---

[10] Ecclesiastes 12:13
[11] Isaiah 11:1–3

enjoyed the persecution He endured, or looked forward to the suffering of the cross. Rather:

> *And he withdrew from them about a stone's throw, and knelt down and prayed, saying, "Father, if you are willing, remove this cup from me. Nevertheless, not my will, but yours, be done." And there appeared to him an angel from heaven, strengthening him. And being in agony he prayed more earnestly; and his sweat became like great drops of blood falling down to the ground.*[12]

Truly, He set the example, and none of us will ever be required to suffer as He did. That said, we do deal with the problem of inherited sin, also known as generational sin or iniquity. With that first sin in Eden, not only did fear enter into everyone's generational line, but so did the false expectations that are defined by our perceived want, need and lack. With that in mind, the next chapter deals with the subject of generational iniquity.

---

[12] Luke 22:41–44

CHAPTER TWELVE:
WHAT'S ALL THIS GENERATIONAL STUFF?

It's a question that is often asked, but scripture sets the stage for the answer:

> *You shall not bow down to them or serve them, for I the* LORD *your God am a jealous God, visiting the iniquity of the fathers on the children to the third and the fourth generation of those who hate me, but showing steadfast love to thousands of those who love me and keep my commandments.* [1]

We believe the issue of generational iniquity is best illustrated in the familiar story of Cain.[2] Let's review. Cain and his brother Abel brought a sacrifice to the Lord; Abel's sacrifice was found worthy in God's eyes, while Cain's was not. This story marks an important distinction between sin, rebellion and iniquity. When Cain became angry, sad and dejected, the Lord said to Cain, "Sin crouches at your door; its desire is for you, but you must master it." In response to this, Cain did three things. First, and perhaps most profoundly, he departed from the presence of the Lord. Next, he convinced his brother to come out to the fields, where he killed him. Lastly, when the Lord asked him

---

[1] Exodus 20:5–6
[2] Genesis 4:1-16

where his brother was, Cain replied, "Am I my brother's keeper?" And after this answer, the Lord cursed Cain.

We may define sin simply as separation from God, and Cain's departing from the presence of the Lord exemplifies this. In the Old Testament, the law required sin offerings for such things as coming in contact with a dead animal carcass or a dead body, so we can see that sin occurs from actions as simple as taking our eyes off God and going astray; there is not necessarily any malicious intent. Rebellion, on the other hand, occurs when we knowingly do that which God has commanded us and charged us not to do, when we do it anyway.

For generational issues, however, iniquity becomes our primary concern, and Cain's answer to God exemplifies iniquity. The Lord asked Cain, "Where is your brother?" and Cain didn't not say, "Lord, I have sinned greatly, for I have committed murder upon my own brother." He didn't even respond rebelliously, "Listen, I know it's against the rules, but I killed Abel, so could we just get this punishment thing over with, Lord?" Instead, he replied, "Am I my brother's keeper?" Cain gave an answer that distorted the truth; he chose not to confess the truth with contrition, nor to tell the truth, albeit without remorse, but his answer was crafted to cover his sin and rebellion, evading consequences altogether. Thus, we may define iniquity as a twisted response to God. The Hebrew word *avown* is translated here as iniquity, and this word comes from the root word *avah*, which Strong's translates as, "do amiss, bow down, make crooked, pervert." God cursed Cain for his actions, and Cain replied, "My punishment is too great!" The word translated as 'punishment' is actually *avown*; so Cain was quite literally saying, "My crookedness is too great." 'Crookedness' may refer to either his own crooked ways, the punishment that comes with them, or both. Quite literally then, this crookedness is visited upon the sons (future generations) in the sense of the curse, encompassing not only the punishment but also the sense of the distorted response.

Let's get some perspective. The Father sent His Son, Jesus, to atone once and for all for our sins on the cross. He bore the weight of all our sins; He became a curse for us, so that we might have freedom. He has completely conquered sin forever. He alone could bear it; the victory is His. The Apostle Paul wrote:

> *I have been crucified with Christ. It is no longer I who live, but Christ who lives in me. And the life I now live in the flesh I live by faith in the Son of God, who loved me and gave himself for me.*[3]

If we can become as Paul described, so that it is not me who lives, but Christ in me, then we can carry His victory in us. We believe the Father visits the iniquity of the fathers on the sons, not because He has a heart to burden people but so that they may be confronted with this twisting of the truth and rise to the challenge and overcome it. None of this is through our own righteousness, but through the righteous sacrifice of the One Who lives in us, Jesus. In this way, the

---

[3] Galatians 2:20

sons may be presented with a wrong response, perceive the sin, and be given the opportunity that their fathers squandered to master it:

> *The one who conquers will be clothed thus in white garments, and I will never blot his name out of the book of life. I will confess his name before my Father and before his angels.*[4]

Great is the reward promised for those who persevere and learn to overcome.

But that's Old Testament! Yes. That is exactly where it is.

Consider this question: What is a Testament? The American Heritage Dictionary defines it as 'something that serves as tangible proof or evidence'. It comes from the Latin word *testis*, which can be translated roughly to mean 'witness'. Who or what does the Old Testament give evidence of? Who or what is it a witness to? You're probably already rolling your eyes because, of course, it is God to Whom the Old Testament gives witness. Please don't shrug this aside; it's the reason we still carry all those pages around in our Bibles. The testament may be old, but as for the God of Whom it testifies, <u>He is still the same</u>. He does not change. If doubt still lingers about the relevance of the Old Testament, consider Jesus' stunning words in His parable about the rich man and Lazarus, the beggar:

---

[4] Revelation 3:5

But Abraham said, "They have Moses and the Prophets;
let them hear them." And he said, "No, father Abraham,
but if someone goes to them from the dead, they will
repent." He said to him, "If they do not hear Moses and
the Prophets, neither will they be convinced if someone
should rise from the dead." [5]

For those who find themselves echoing the objection about
generational iniquity being confined to the Old Testament,
consider: Gal 5:3-4, which says this:

I testify again to every man who accepts circumcision
that he is obligated to keep the whole law. 4 You are
severed from Christ, you who would be justified by the
law; you have fallen away from grace.[6]

Much of the Old Testament, though not all by any means,
describes God's commands to the Israelites; in other words,
it deals with the law. Yet, even in the Old Testament, God
expressed His contempt for songs, offerings and festivals
because of the people's attitude, though all of these were in
keeping with the law. In fact, the Lord almost killed Balaam
for having a wrong attitude and being spiritually
insensitive, even though he was following the command of
the Lord. Apostle Paul exhorted us not to try and work out
our salvation through the law:

---

[5] Luke 16:29–31
[6] Galatians 5:3–4

So then, the law was our guardian until Christ came, in order that we might be justified by faith.[7]

Why then the law? It was added because of transgressions, until the offspring should come to whom the promise had been made, and it was put in place through angels by an intermediary.[8]

So then you are no longer strangers and aliens, but you are fellow citizens with the saints and members of the household of God, **built on the foundation of the apostles and prophets, Christ Jesus himself being the cornerstone,** *in whom the whole structure, being joined together, grows into a holy temple in the Lord.*[9]

Get that? We are His house, built on the foundation of the apostles and the prophets, and the cornerstone is Christ Jesus Himself (bold added for emphasis).

While God never changes, He can and has changed His commands in keeping with His time or season. Acts 11 describes how He repealed His commands to only eat the flesh of certain animals just before the first Gentiles received the Spirit, and Paul fervently urged the brethren against circumcision:

---

[7] Galatians 3:24.
[8] Galatians 3:19
[9] Ephesians 2:19–21

Look: I, Paul, say to you that if you accept circumcision, Christ will be of no advantage to you. [10]

Exodus 20:5, which describes generational iniquity, includes no commandment; it's not the law. It is not even an impersonal, categorical description of how God's legal system works, such as, "The wages of sin are death." Exodus 20:5 describes God! Read it again:

...for I the LORD your God am a jealous God, visiting the iniquity of the fathers on the children to the third and the fourth generation of those who hate me, but showing steadfast love to thousands of those who love me and keep my commandments.

This describes not the law, but a characteristic of God's ways and His justice. The Lord loves righteousness right now just as much as He did in the days of Adam. He still does not despise those with a contrite heart and a broken spirit; and although He sent Jesus to be a friend to sinners and release us from sin's bondage, He still hates sin. What He tells us to do may depend on context, but His character does not change.

Lest there be any confusion about the subject of generational sin in our New Covenant times, consider the words of the Lord: Luke 11:47-51 (Amplified):

Woe to you! For you are rebuilding and repairing the tombs of the prophets, whom your fathers killed

---

[10] Galatians 5:2

(destroyed). So you bear witness and give your full approval and consent to the deeds of your fathers; for they actually killed them, and you rebuild and repair monuments to them. For this reason also the wisdom of God said, I will send them prophets and apostles, [some] of whom they will put to death and persecute, so that the blood of all the prophets shed from the foundation of the world may be charged against and required of this age and generation, from the blood of Abel to the blood of Zechariah, who was slain between the altar and the sanctuary. Yes, I tell you, it shall be charged against and required of this age and generation.[11]

Clearly, Jesus is explicitly telling us that as these sons faced the sins of their fathers, they could be held accountable for them according to their responses. The Pharisees chose to honor the prophets in much the same way that they honored Jesus; with their mouths, while their hearts were far from Him. The word hypocrisy comes from the word for 'actor', or 'play-acting'. The honor of the Pharisees was just an act, which they performed so that they would be seen honoring Jesus and the prophets. They were courting the favor of the people and seeking to be esteemed by those who really did love Jesus and the prophets. They loved the honor of men, and they loved for men to bow down to them in public.

---

[11] Luke 11:47-51, *Amplified Bible Classic Edition* (AMPC) Copyright © 1954, 1958, 1962, 1964, 1965, 1987 by The Lockman Foundation

Deep generational iniquity was being passed down from their fathers, and they chose to treat only the outside. They were coating that sin, and sealing it in with a thick lacquer of whitewash. I know the following sounds cheeky, but I mean it quite literally and sincerely: If you have issues with a generational paradigm, please take them up with the Lord. Romans 14:23 teaches that whatever does not originate and proceed from faith is sin, so until the day arrives when the Lord allows you to accept a generational paradigm on faith, we will have to live in patience:

> *Let not the one who eats despise the one who abstains, and let not the one who abstains pass judgment on the one who eats, for God has welcomed him. Who are you to pass judgment on the servant of another? It is before his own master that he stands or falls. And he will be upheld, for the Lord is able to make him stand.* [12]

Until that day, we'll just have to believe in a great God, Who stands far above and beyond all the ways of men, and Who accepts all kinds of people, just for having faith in Jesus Christ.

Okay, I get the idea, but so what?

So, we know that iniquity can be passed down through the generations, thus the term, 'generational iniquity'; and we have a very vague idea of what it looks like because we can conceive a seemingly infinite number of scenarios that might indicate the presence of generational iniquity.

---

[12] Romans 14:3–4

Generally though, we look for patterns of destruction and devouring occurring pervasively and repeatedly within a family. From here, we do something which we call, 'identificational repentance', a big term that simply means we:

1. Perceive, through the Spirit, the presence of the twistedness, the iniquity

2. Identify with those in our family line who fell into this sin (as in Daniel 9)

3. Confess it as sin

4. Place that sin in the hands of Jesus on the cross

5. Turn away from it and turn back to God (repent)

We also ask the Lord to remove the curses and consequences that resulted from that iniquity. In other words, the process is the same process of repentance described repeatedly by the prophets, and for that matter, by Jesus. The only wrinkle unique to identificational repentance is that we intentionally choose to identify with those in our family line, rather than acting like the Pharisee who says, "Thank you, God, that you didn't make me like that sinner." God expressed His heart for this kind of repentance clearly:

But if they confess their iniquity and the iniquity of their fathers in their treachery that they committed against me, and also in walking contrary to me.[13]

In this way, we can work out our salvation through fear and trembling.[14]

We must be careful, however, as we walk through this process, to rely on the guidance of the Holy Spirit, for we cannot conquer iniquity through our own power or might, but only by His Spirit, Who is released to us through our faith in Jesus. I write this as an aside, but please, let my words implore you to understand this as the primary and the most important caveat of all. Do what you must to get this imprinted in your mind. Picture a drill sergeant; and then imagine the sound of thunder booming through the words as you re-read them: **Rely on the Holy Spirit!**

So, the long story short of it all is to identify with those who committed the sin, and then repent under the leadership of the Holy Spirit. I emphasize this again because we cannot manipulate God. He is indeed Jehovah Rapha; [15] He is indeed healing; He is the liberation we seek. But we cannot force His hand into acting in a particular manner by means of our actions, formulas, procedures or protocols. He does it because He wants to, because He is our Father and He loves us so much that He sent His Son, Jesus, to bear all of

---

[13] Leviticus 26:40
[14] Philippians 2:12
[15] Jehovah Rapha means the God Who Heals

the weight that we cannot. He does not act because we found the secret formula to force His hand; neither does He act because of our own merits; He acts because of Who He is.

> For while we were still weak, at the right time Christ died for the ungodly. For one will scarcely die for a righteous person — though perhaps for a good person one would dare even to die — but God shows his love for us in that while we were still sinners, Christ died for us.[16]

---

[16] Romans 5:6–8

CHAPTER THIRTEEN:
HEALING HELPS

We understand that every difficulty that has been raised regarding fear and staying on the ancient paths may not be quickly or easily overcome, so here we offer some suggestions. Isaiah wrote:

> *A voice cries: "In the wilderness prepare the way of the LORD; make straight in the desert a highway for our God.[1]*

This is the goal, a direct path to the Lord that is level and free of all obstructions from both personal and generational iniquity; but the sad fact is that fear, that first human response to sin, gets in the way all too often. The destruction of fear and its associated evils traps us in ungodly dimensional places. Often, it can be dealt with by means of generational prayer, and we recommend:

- *Prayer to Release One From the Ungodly Depth[2]*

- *Prayer to be Removed From the Ungodly Width[3]*

- *Prayer to Reject Deception About Our Position in Christ[4]*

---

[1] Isaiah 40:3
[2] aslansplace.com/prayer-to-release-one-from-the-ungodly-depth/
[3] aslansplace.com/prayer-to-be-removed-from-the-ungodly-width/
[4] aslansplace.com/prayer-to-reject-deception-about-our-position-in-christ/

- *Prayer to Abolish Fear[5]*

- *Prayer to Restore Compassion and the Fear of the Lord[6]*

- *Prayer to Remove the Effects of the Ungodly Mighty Ones[7]*

Another resource that is very helpful is *Swatting the Fly of Fear*.[8]

Think back to the report from Dr Earl Henslin in Chapter Two (pages 23-24), which indicated that the level of agitation in the brain decreases (as compared to a baseline brain scan) when remaining in the presence of the Holy Spirit. This is scientific validation of a spiritual truth:

May the God of hope fill you with all joy and peace in believing, so that by the power of the Holy Spirit you may abound in hope.[9]

And the peace of God, which surpasses all understanding, will guard your hearts and your minds in Christ Jesus. Finally, brothers, whatever is true, whatever is honorable, whatever is just, whatever is pure, whatever is lovely, whatever is commendable, if there is any excellence, if there is anything worthy of praise, think about these things. [9] What you have learned and

---

[5] aslansplace.com/prayer-to-abolish-fear/
[6] aslansplace.com/prayer-to-restore-compassion-and-the-fear-of-the-lord/
[7] aslansplace.com/remove-ungodly-mighty-ones/
[8] aslansplace.com/swatting-the-fly-of-fear/
[9] Romans 15:13

received and heard and seen in me — practice these things, and the God of peace will be with you. [10]

It is important to remember that fear and its by-products may also have a physical component. OMIM®[11] identifies the following ailments along with the number of entries for each:

- Fear — 127

- Anxiety — 305

- Fear Caused — 9,500

- Fear Compared — 6,693

- Fear Conditioning — 174

- Fear Conditioning — 6,712

- Fear Conditioning Drives — 689

- Fear Conditioning Compared — 4,374

- Fear Conditioning Induced — 2,339

- Fear Conditioning Leads — 2,951

- Anxiety Attacks — 658

- Anxiety Behavior — 1,468

---

[10] Philippians 4:7–9
[11] omim.org

- Anxiety Paralleled – 1,544

- Anxiety Compared – 6,780

- Anxiety Deficits – 1,401

- Anxiety Disorders – 8,854

- Anxiety Disorders Compared – 11,853

- Panic – 40

- Panic Anxiety – 320

- Panic Anxiety Compared – 6,788

- Panic attacks – 402

- Panic Disorder – 8,809

- Panic Disorder Patients – 13,495

- Panic Disorder Resulted – 11,906

- Panic Disorder Segregated – 9,647

- Panic Disorder Showed – 18,816

- Phobia Carried – 2,694

Overwhelmed by a little too much detail? Just think how much worse it gets if we were to add in such infirmities as depression, gastro-intestinal problems, immune responses and migraines, not to mention a host of others with fear at their root. One should not hesitate to seek medical help when dealing with any such persistent issues.

Certainly, the Bible validates the importance of prayers for healing, and the *Prayer For DNA* and *Ministering to the DNA & How To Locate a Problem on a Chromosome*[12] is often very helpful.

Dr Henslin has shared that in the bone marrow, a principle component of the immune system, there is a marker with one tip in the marrow and one in the brain (the DNA). It's the way we are wired, so to speak. Furthermore, there is biblical evidence that prayer helps to improve the immune system, evidence that once again illustrates how the Bible only validates true science; it doesn't contradict it.

> *For when I kept silent, my bones wasted away through my groaning all day long. For day and night your hand was heavy upon me; my strength was dried up as by the heat of summer. Selah*
>
> *I acknowledged my sin to you, and I did not cover my iniquity; I said, "I will confess my transgressions to the* LORD*," and you forgave the iniquity of my sin. Selah* [13]

The ultimate cure for all that ails us is the blood of Jesus, His work at the cross. Intimacy with Him is the pathway that will take us ever deeper into His complete healing. It is the pathway that takes up into His righteous Deep, where the

---

[12] aslansplace.com/prayer-for-dna/
[13] Psalms 32:3–5

deep things of God call out to the deep things of mankind in communion of Spirit to spirit:

> Deep calls to deep at the roar of your waterfalls; all your breakers and your waves have gone over me. By day the LORD commands his steadfast love, and at night his song is with me, a prayer to the God of my life. [14]

---

[14] Psalms 42:7–8

CHAPTER FOURTEEN:
NEW EXPECTATIONS

God is not like a trained pet who can be expected to perform on demand. Not only that, but He is endlessly creative in the manner by which He accomplishes things. Even the Church hasn't learned this lesson well; too often, we keep looking back at previous revivals or successful programs, attempting to duplicate those previous moves of God. But, we simply cannot confine God or His ways in a box:

> *For my thoughts are not your thoughts, neither are your ways my ways, declares the* LORD. *For as the heavens are higher than the earth, so are my ways higher than your ways and my thoughts than your thoughts.*[1]

Since our expectations are often built upon perceptions gained from personal experiences, they are not necessarily an absolute reality. Remember, the ungodly cycle of want, need, and lack manifests in expectations that are tainted by deception. Looking into our archives of prophetic words, it's a bit surprising to see just how often He has encouraged us to not only lay those expectations down, but also to expect new things from Him. In other words, lay down the old God-boxes and let Him out so He can deliver on His promises through righteous expectations, through faith. Some of those words:

---

[1] Isaiah 55:8–9

2007: Lay down your expectations. Let me be your expectations. Expect me to manifest my glory. Lay down all other expectations. Have I not always come through? Have I not always supplied? I have been with you in the valley and in the mountaintop. Would I ever leave you? Would I ever forsake you? Let this be a test of faith. No expectations. Just walk with me. Walk with me. For I am God. I am the one who has never forsaken you.

2007: And I desire to draw you unto myself. I desire to draw you onto myself. I long for more intimacy. Lay down your expectations. Lay down your agendas. Give me free reign. Let us play like children. Lay down your boxes. Learn about each other. Come to me. I long for you.

2008: The establisher has come again. There is a new living way; I will break your old ways of doing things, seeing things, hearing things. Expectancy, without it you are not going to get there; but when expectancy meets Jesus, who is Love, then expectancy is fulfilled. When expectancy has reached its fullness of time, then birth takes place. This about birth, rebirth and new birth; they are triplets. The beginning becomes the end, which becomes the beginning; Old things are passed away, all things are new. First the rest, then the unity, and then the expectancy. Then the birth, rebirth and new birth.

2009: My dear children I am so pleased with you. That you are spending yourselves in coming here to be filled up with more; you came here expecting. I am encouraging you to expect even more. Expect the unexpected. Believe for the impossible. For each one of you, know that the favor of God is surrounding you and resting upon you. I tell you that in a time of favor, ask for more. I see many, many doors opening. This morning you sang to me with a grateful heart, but I want you to know that My heart is full for each one of you. Fasten your seat belts, be expecting. Share!

2009: We don't have an expectancy of how good God is, and what He wants to do. We can't win the race unless we expect to win the race. We have to stir it up with expectancy. Even when we sin, He knew ahead of time. He is going to work it for good; we have to expect, expect, expect. Stir up expectancy. He said He is good and yes; He is goodness and compassion. Everything is planned for us to prosper, to do good, to be good, to be all that He has for us.

In 2012, we met together as a very small group for what became the first of six progressively larger yearly summits. Portions of our exploration during that meeting are included below, with each paragraph indicating a different person speaking:

I sense a very large angel over with a message; it's a territorial angel over the Victor Valley. (This is where Aslan's Place is located)

It feels like there's something to dig out, like there's an obstacle to clear away. It feels like there's a whole bunch of clutter in the spirit; the mindsets have produced a bunch of clutter that has built up in order to get to a different destination. I'm hearing that the angel is here to assist. An analogy would be like the frequencies getting clogged with signals, as in a cell phone.

(Prayed to disentangle wrong associations that would cause clutter from Aslan's Place.)

What is the purpose of this summit?

God is refining His people. He's taken some out of this group, and there's going to be a lot of resistance. The group that He's calling us to is part of a higher calling, a higher place, a more disciplined place, and a lonelier walk. The falling off of some of the people will be painful, but you need to be very discerning of who is to be around you.

We're following the cloud, not the crowd.

We ain't going where He ain't blowing.

What do you say when people ask if you're part of Aslan's Place? The response I've had is that it's where my heart is connected. My sense is that now, rather than being the way it was, it's a new thing we are part of and connected to; and Aslan's Place is where we come together and go up the mountain, and then take it home to our different ministries.

Yes, and each ministry does it their own way.

Are there deposits that need to be removed?

I have a sense that there are deposits of 'yucky' stuff here.

It's all of the expectations that were deposited onto Aslan's Place.

Last night I kept experiencing the ungodly depths. I wonder if these ungodly expectations have placed Aslan's Place in the ungodly depths.

Paul prayed, asking the Lord to remove us from entrapments, snares, etc.

We need to ask for everything that has been stolen to be returned.

This morning when I was worshipping, the angel of provision showed up. Father, we what you have revealed to flow down the mountain to Aslan's Place.

I'm still stuck on deposits. Are there legal transactions that need to be considered? Are there gates that have been compromised by ungodly trading of that which people have received from Paul or Aslan's Place?

Paul responded, "Any way that I've agreed to ungodly trading, I renounce that, and where others have traded with me for position, I also renounce that.

I think that's huge, there is something that is still surrounding the property.

Paul again, "Lord, remove all the IOUs'; I do not owe them anything; I don't owe them a name, favor, position, entitlements or recognition.

(The spiritual atmosphere changed.)

Righteous expectancy increasingly became a part of our day-to-day expectancy; and the Lord grew those summits, which began with five people in 2012, to over fifty in 2017. But then He told Paul, "This is the last one," much to the disappointment of many. But God is God, and He had other methods of ministry on His agenda, which He has continually used to blow our minds; we are routinely awestruck by what He's done now and look forward with righteous expectancy of what He will do next.

What might have happened had Paul insisted on keeping God in our box of expectations? Only God knows, but it cannot be denied that revelation has escalated beyond anything we could have imagined, which is undoubtedly due a great deal to obedience. Only in retrospect while writing this chapter, does the timing become clear. The very first *Exploring Heavenly Places* book was completed and published about six months after that first summit.

We can always expect that God will be faithful to His promises:

> *Know therefore that the* LORD *your God is God, the faithful God who keeps covenant and steadfast love with those who love him and keep his commandments, to a thousand generations*[2]

> *God is not man, that he should lie, or a son of man, that he should change his mind. Has he said, and will he not do it? Or has he spoken, and will he not fulfill it?* [3]

> *I will also praise you with the harp for your faithfulness, O my God; I will sing praises to you with the lyre, O Holy One of Israel.* [4]

And so as we finish, we arrive back where we began with the Preface, "Peace is not a place; it's not a state of mind that one achieves; peace is a person, and His name is Jesus Christ":

> *For to us a child is born, to us a son is given; and the government shall be upon his shoulder, and his name shall be called Wonderful Counselor, Mighty Everlasting Father, Prince of Peace. Of the increase*

---

[2] Deuteronomy 7:9
[3] Numbers 23:19
[4] Psalms 71:22

of his government and of peace there will be no end, on the throne of David and over his kingdom to establish it and to uphold it with justice and with righteousness from this time forth and forevermore. The zeal of the Lord of hosts will do this.[5]

Peace I leave with you; my peace I give to you. Not as the world gives do I give to you. Let not your hearts be troubled, neither let them be afraid.[6]

As we conclude, we offer one final prayer to assist in the journey out of fear and ungodly expectations:

Prayer to be Released from Ungodly Want, Need, Lack and Expectations

On behalf of myself and my family line, I repent for settling into a mindset of lack, of always wanting, needing and expecting something else, rather than trusting You. I repent for not believing that You are always good and Your lovingkindness endures forever. Lord, please take me out of the ungodly dimensions where want, need, lack and expect reside. Place me into Your kingdom mindset, for I want to be a kingdom-oriented person who sees Your kingdom come on earth as it is in Heaven. I declare that I do not have to operate in lack; I don't always have to experience want or need regarding

---

[5] Isaiah 9:6-7
[6] John 14:27

what I don't have; and I can expect You to always do what's right. I will not only be content, but also will contend for everything You want me to have.

Lord, I surrender any personal or generational resistance over to You. I give You permission to release into me a desire to create, to see those things that are not as they should be. Help me to comprehend Your desire for me to live in abundance, prosperity and fruitfulness through Your limitless design. Sanctify my imagination to call those things into place that You intend for my family, for influence, for creative finances and prosperity.

Enlighten the eyes of my heart, Lord, in Jesus' name.

CONCLUSION

As it has turned out, the statement in the Preface, "By the time this book is published, the pandemic will hopefully be history," was indeed hopeful. In California where we live, the shutdown is still very much a reality, even though restrictions in many other states have been largely removed. It seems like the enemy is milking Covid-19 for all it is worth in his attempt to instill fear, destroy faith and shut down God's Church. But you see, the enemy doesn't seem to understand that the true Church is not confined to buildings, but is the living, breathing Body of Christ.[1] God's people will not succumb to persecution any more now than they did during the days of Acts when Roman persecution caused them to scatter to the ends of the known world. Today, new buds of the Lord's harvest[2] appear to be blossoming very quickly in spite of Covid-19 and/or anything else that evil is doing to try to prevent it.

How interesting that our stated goal for this volume of *Exploring Heavenly Places* was, "to further equip God's people to persevere and endure within a worldly system that wants nothing more than to snuff out Christianity." Little did we know that we were about to see that happen to a greater extent than ever before in the United States of America.

---

[1] 1 Corinthians 12:27, Romans 12:4-5
[2] Luke 10:2, John 4:35

Our prayer now is that the insights shared in this book will help strengthen our readers to live in the Rest of the Lord; to dwell in His peace, despite whatever trials may come during these days as His return rapidly approaches. The words of the angels when He departed leave us with an unshakable hope for what is looming on the horizon:

> *"Men of Galilee, why do you stand looking into heaven? This Jesus, who was taken up from you into heaven, will come in the same way as you saw him go into heaven."* [3]

To be honest, our subtitle, *The Mystery of the Ancient Paths,* is only a teaser for the far more extensive mysteries that God wants to reveal within the heart of each believer. He is beyond understanding, and there's always more to learn:

> *Oh, the depth of the riches and wisdom and knowledge of God! How unsearchable are his judgments and how inscrutable his ways!* [4]

As we travel along His ancient pathways of discovery, we can know that peace and rest along our journey is guaranteed by Jesus' own words:

> *Come to me, all who labor and are heavy laden, and I will give you rest. Take my yoke upon you, and learn from me, for I am gentle and lowly in heart, and you will find*

---

[3] Acts 1:11
[4] Romans 11:33–36

rest for your souls. For my yoke is easy, and my burden is light." [5]

These things I have spoken to you while I am still with you. But the Helper, the Holy Spirit, whom the Father will send in my name, he will teach you all things and bring to your remembrance all that I have said to you. Peace I leave with you; my peace I give to you. Not as the world gives do I give to you. Let not your hearts be troubled, neither let them be afraid. You heard me say to you, 'I am going away, and I will come to you.' If you loved me, you would have rejoiced, because I am going to the Father, for the Father is greater than I. And now I have told you before it takes place, so that when it does take place you may believe. [6]

May the Lord bless your journey along His ancient paths and into His Rest; may He reveal His individually personalized mysteries to your heart and mind.

---

[5] Matthew 11:28–30
[6] John 14:25–29

Made in United States
Cleveland, OH
12 July 2025

18507940R00075